PROVIDENCE
WAS
WITH
US

JAPAN LIBRARY

Water being sent through the Gamberi cross-desert canal. (August 2009.)

Three and a half years after the Gamberi cross-desert canal first opened. (May 2013.)

Cultivation of the Gamberi Desert. (March 2010.)

Gamberi Harvest. (April 2011.)

The scene after water has begun to flow. The water is being sent from terminus Q4 along the bedrock into the Gamberi cross-desert canal. (August 10, 2009.)

The Gamberi Desert nearly ten years after the canal's completion. (April 27, 2019.)

PROVIDENCE WAS WITH US

How a Japanese Doctor
Turned the Afghan Desert Green

NAKAMURA Tetsu

Translated by Carl Freire

Japan Publishing Industry Foundation for Culture

Note on Japanese names and geographic names:
Japanese personal names in this book are spelled in accordance with the bearer's wishes where known; otherwise they are romanized according to the Hepburn system, with long vowels indicated by macrons. The names are given in Japanese order, family name first.
Geographic names without a standard romanized spelling have been rendered according to guidance from local authorities.

Providence Was with Us: How a Japanese Doctor Turned the Afghan Desert Green
Nakamura Tetsu. Translated by Carl Freire.

Published by
Japan Publishing Industry Foundation for Culture (JPIC)
2-2-30 Kanda-Jinbocho, Chiyoda-ku, Tokyo 101-0051, Japan

First English edition: December 2020

This book is a translation of *Ten, tomo ni ari: Afuganisutan sanjūnen no tatakai* (NHK Publishing, Inc., 2013).
English publishing rights arranged with the heir to the literary estate of the author.

Book design: Miki Kazuhiko, Ampersand Works

Printed in Japan
ISBN 978-4-86658-147-7
https://japanlibrary.jpic.or.jp/

"In Truth, Who Destroys Me?"

On December 4, 2019, Dr. Nakamura Tetsu was slain in a hail of bullets fired by a band of unknown assailants as he was traveling from his lodgings in Jalalabad, Afghanistan, to an irrigation canal work site. This utterly devastating event has called attention to the activities—providing medical care, working to construct irrigation canals for farmers, and contributing to Afghanistan's reconstruction through the revival of the country's agricultural sector—that have made him esteemed so highly by people in Japan and around the world.

As the general director of Peace Japan Medical Services (PMS) and representative of the Peshawar-kai in Afghanistan, Dr. Nakamura had been known to people of good will in Japan and Afghanistan. Elsewhere he had attracted little attention prior to his assassination, but news of this incident served to raise his international profile. Reports ran in such varied media as *The Lancet* ("Obituary: Tetsu Nakamura," vol. 395, no. 10219, January 18, 2020) and the *Financial Times* ("A Japanese saint among the sinners of the Afghan war," January 1, 2020). I believe that this coverage finally made people around the world realize that his work had been there all along, flowing like an underground river; this knowledge touched their hearts profoundly.

Dr. Nakamura published around a dozen books describing his activities, but other than one technical report on the methods that were used to build the Marwarid irrigation canal, nothing has been published in English. That report, *The Afghan Green Ground Project* (2018), appeared in Japanese, English, Dari, and Pashtun. It discussed the essence of "reviving agriculture with irrigation construction methods learned from tradition," but since the text was written for project managers and focused on local farmers, it did not catch the eye of the general public.

In 2013, Dr. Nakamura published an autobiographical work in Japanese discussing his early years, his work as a physician in Pakistan and Afghanistan, and his biggest project, the construction of the Marwarid Canal. I believe the publication of the English-language edition of that book will enable people everywhere to learn not only about Dr. Nakamura's accomplishments but also how the experience of carrying out these projects influenced his outlook and gave rise to profound insights.

After his formative training as a physician in Japan, Dr. Nakamura's international activities began in 1984 with his participation in a Hansen's disease eradication program in Peshawar, a city in northwestern Pakistan close to the Afghan border. Over the years, he shifted his focus from the practice of medicine to the supply of water and ultimately to the revival of agriculture. Through all his work, which bridged the Afghanistan-Pakistan border, he helped sustain the lives of refugees and farmers. Afghanistan was being ravaged not only by war but also by drought. Dr. Nakamura restored life to the parched earth with irrigation facilities built using techniques he developed with his own ingenuity and creativity.

Thanks to Dr. Nakamura's efforts, water drawn from the Kunar River has turned 16,500 hectares of eastern Afghanistan into a fertile plain that provides a place for 600,000 farmers and their families to go about their lives. The project he launched and led is now seen as a model for Afghan reconstruction. The full picture of how that happened is presented in this book.

I suspect it was difficult for the translators to convey how Dr. Nakamura expressed himself with writing that is both simple and yet quietly and deeply stirring. The reality of the situations behind his words was deadly serious in some cases. And there were matters that he chose not to talk much about. But in the preface to this book he expresses two thoughts that to me seem to convey the essence of his message. "I can hardly begin to assess the human bonds that fate has sent my way," he writes. And then, "So long as we recognize we cannot do everything we want to do and are honest and faithful," he declares, "we can rely on what heaven provides and on the sincerity of others." If this book allows readers to understand the weightiness of the experiences that led Dr. Nakamura to these thoughts, it will help them understand why his activities were so significant.

Dr. Nakamura wrote this book at a point when his work in Afghanistan was reaching maturity. The impetus for him to undertake his work in the first place arose from his experience serving as the team physician for a mountaineering expedition that climbed Tirich Mir, the highest peak in the Hindu Kush mountains, in 1978. In his 1992 book *Peshawāru nite* (At Peshawar), he wrote about the outcome of that trip: "It was as though a chain of curious bonds drew me back to the North-West Frontier Province five years later. Taking up my new job there was a consequence of the shock I experienced on my first visit to the Hindu Kush. It was also a way for me to avenge the absurdity of such excessive inequality." There is a fury to how he expressed himself. Reading that book, I recognize that Dr. Nakamura's anger at the inequities accompanying poverty and his empathy for the downtrodden coursed strongly throughout everything he did.

After an extremist faction of the Taliban blasted the stone Buddhist statues of Bamyan in 2001, Dr. Nakamura wrote the following in a piece for the *Asahi Shimbun* (April 3):

> When I saw the great Buddha in Bamyan with only part of its body remaining, for some reason that heartbreaking appearance delivered a revelation to me. "In truth, who destroys me?" The silence of that immense rock, even shattered into innumerable pieces, conveyed the determination of someone who had passed away carrying the weight of all human foolishness on their shoulders, and who was still trying to rouse the Buddha-nature that resides in everyone. It struck me as divine. In its indifference to the clamorous world of humans, it also seemed to be showing me a definite something.

I cannot help feeling that Dr. Nakamura—whom we have now lost—exemplifies the very nobility evinced by this great Buddha.

Murakami Masaru
Chairman, Peshawar-kai
General Director, Peace Japan Medical Services (PMS)

Bonds of Fate

This book looks back over the thirty years that I, a doctor from Japan, have spent conducting various activities in Afghanistan. It presents a picture of why I started to undertake my work here, and why I started to devote my energies to the tasks of digging wells and building canals for irrigation beyond my medical practice. It is based on the transcript of a television program about my activities that was aired by NHK, Japan's public broadcaster, in June–July 2006. I have edited the text and added content covering the years up to the time of this writing (2013). Accordingly, this book includes details about more recent developments in the Afghan situation and in my own activities, but the basic subject remains the same.

The retaliatory strikes launched by the US military in October 2001, in the wake of the September 11 terrorist attacks, and the subsequent "Afghan revival" that followed the collapse of the Taliban regime were widely covered in the Japanese and other foreign media. Since then, though the strife has continued, the illusion has taken hold that Afghanistan has somehow settled down, and the country seems to have been forgotten. But what is happening here right now? The great drought that is being suffered in Afghanistan even today remains largely unknown internationally. Once a self-sufficient agricultural country where 90 percent of the population were farmers and nomads, Afghanistan is now in a critical state. I wonder why it is that people are not fully aware of this grave situation, and I cannot help but feel that this indifference is a sign of how sick our world may be.

I have said over and over again in my other writings that all of the contradictions and sufferings that exist in Asia can be found in Afghanistan. However, I sense we are now at the point where the troubles facing this distant country—which is confronting the reality of desertification caused by climate change—are in fact being cast into sharp relief as problems that Japan shares, namely, environmental concerns and the issues of war and peace.

⸎

As I look back, I can hardly begin to assess the human bonds that fate has sent my way over the past thirty years of my life. And if I were to faithfully trace all the developments that led me to where I am today, I would have to run through the numerous encounters that I have had since childhood.

We humans lament our misfortunes and rejoice in our good luck, and over and over it is the pleasures or anxieties close at hand that grab our interest. We often ignore the providence of nature and are inclined to labor under the illusion that we have freedom and rights that allow us to act as we please. It strikes me that people today have an inflated sense of their place in the world, subscribing to the concept of freedom of desire and placing their faith in science and technology, with the result that they take both life and nature too lightly.

⸎

Where you wind up in life is determined by the people you meet and the events that come your way, and your responses to such encounters. The happenings in our lives, however small, are broadly and organically connected to one another by bonds that transcend time and place. And I cannot help but sense that there is something sacred that goes beyond the realm of human intentions. In a world of such wide-ranging bonds, every life has meaning. We just may not be able to see it. This is something that I want people to realize.

What I can say, after having lived in Afghanistan for thirty years, is that so long as we recognize we cannot do everything we want to do and are honest and faithful, we can rely on what heaven provides and on the sincerity of others. Nothing will make me happier than to have this message help people overcome the common misperceptions of human affairs, get a sense of the blessings we all share, and approach a solid understanding of what we truly need and do not need in this world of uncertainty and violence.

In conclusion, I cannot sufficiently express my gratitude to the many people who have continued for so long to lend their support to our projects on the ground in Afghanistan. Also, I wish to offer my heartfelt apologies and thanks to Mr. Kato Go of NHK Publishing, who so patiently waited for the seven years it took for me to turn the transcript of the television program into the manuscript of the book he asked me to write.

Nakamura Tetsu
General Director, Peace Japan Medical Services (PMS)
October 2013

CONTENTS

Afghanistan, 2009—Mission Accomplished

The Miraculous Workings of Fate

The Gamberi Desert in eastern Afghanistan, which covers an area 4 kilometers across and 20 kilometers long along the border between the eastern Afghanistan provinces of Nangarhar and Laghman, is a beautiful place. But it does not welcome humans. With its hot burning sands, temperatures as high as 53°C, blazing sunlight, and torrid winds, the desert is inhospitable to life of any sort. It is an awe-inspiring revelation that defies description and repels human activity.

On August 3, 2009, four hundred workers were expending the last of their energies in a drive to finish a project in this desert wasteland. Six years and five months after the start of construction in March 2003, the approximately 24-kilometer-long Marwarid Canal had been dug almost to its terminus. The hot winds and sandstorms mercilessly lashed at this cluster of people, who stood out like an isolated dot in the vast expanse of the desert. We had planned to complete the project before the intense heat that would come in April, but the work had proven more difficult than anticipated, resulting in delay after delay. Even though many people collapsed from heat exhaustion every day, the crew had to labor on. If the effort had been halted even temporarily, our schedule for completing the project would undoubtedly have been set back by a year. And on this August day, with just a dozen or so meters to go, the workers were filled with renewed determination to press on to the end.

Late in the morning, the senior worker who was directing the construction of embankments at the terminus reported: "We're almost there. Just a few minutes more. Everyone is tired, but they can last until noon."

And then, finally, the work was done. I said, "OK, let the water flow."

The night before, seeing that we were close to opening the canal, we had filled it with water up to a point 500 meters short of the end. When workers removed the sandbags, water spurted out as if from a burst dam and energetically pushed its way toward the terminus. The flowing water gradually sped up. Slowly but steadily, it filled the channel as it moved forward at a walking pace.

I walked down the 6-meter-wide waterway as if I was guiding the water, and the four hundred workers who had finished their construction work lined the banks, holding their breaths as they watched. There was a final floodgate at the terminus, some 24 kilometers from the intake gate through which the canal draws its water from the Kunar River. It is at the end of the 2.8-kilometer-long channel across the Gamberi Desert. The gate serves the purpose of allowing the overflow from the canal to drop off into the natural floodway below. At noon precisely, the water reached the terminus and forcefully poured down into the floodway. The canal was completely open.

"God is great!"

There was spontaneous cheering and applause, and these men, their bearded faces blackened by the sun, stood transfixed with beaming smiles. The site was abuzz with excitement. This was the product of seven years of sweat and hard work. It was the completion of an irrigation canal that would restore 3,000 hectares of farmland, with the promise of opening up vast new expanses of the Gamberi Desert. The bones of many travelers lay on these sands, and since antiquity people had feared the place as a valley of death. Now it was on its way to becoming a place of lush greenery.

I was among that throng of excited people. As I thought about it, it was amazing that I, a doctor from Japan, had set aside my medical occupation and taken it upon myself to oversee construction of this canal. Though this may have been my destined mission, it was still a peculiar outcome. The fact that I was devoting myself to doing work in a completely different field in this corner of the world suddenly struck me as strange. At the moment we saw the water going through, maybe it was because the tension had been released, but I found myself grinning as I was filled with joy, and I let out a roar of laughter. Twenty-five years before, when I first worked here as a physician, or thirty-one years ago, when I first visited the Hindu Kush range, I never dreamed that I would now be in this place.

⚘

Even today, the path to Afghanistan's reconstruction remains a thorny one. Civil war and the meddling of foreign countries are not the only things that have beaten this country down to its very foundations. The chief culprit is the severe drought that has afflicted the land since summer of the year 2000. Previously this agrarian country was completely self-sufficient in food, and it enriched itself with exports of its agricultural bounty. But its farmland rapidly turned to desert, and more and more villages were abandoned, leading to a rapid increase in the numbers of displaced persons. As a result, food self-sufficiency was cut in half in a mere five years. The drought continues. However, it is the spectacle of war news that gets communicated to the outside world,

The crew works feverishly on the final section of the irrigation canal. (August 2, 2009.)

Workers rejoice at the completion of the canal. (August 3, 2009.)

and hardly any word of the drought is passed on. This is a very important point that I will talk more about later.

Our Peace Japan Medical Services (PMS) group was based in the town of Peshawar in Pakistan, close to the border with Afghanistan, and we had been operating three clinics within Afghanistan since 1991. The region around our Dara-e-Noor Clinic was hit hard by the drought in the summer of 2000, and for some time it went back to being a desert where no trees or plants could survive. The people of the valley abandoned their villages and sought refuge elsewhere. Very quickly, the numbers of children suffering from malnutrition and dehydration rose, and there was no end to deaths from dysentery. Hunger and thirst are not conditions that physicians can cure; addressing these basic needs takes precedence over the practice of medicine. In light of this, I established our Water Management Center in Jalalabad, at the center of Afghanistan's eastern region. Through this center, in parallel with my medical activities, I worked on digging wells to provide people with a source of drinking water, and I helped to improve their irrigation facilities.

Hunger can only be satisfied with food, and producing that food requires water for agriculture. The Marwarid Canal, which would provide water for several thousand hectares and restore greenery, was to be the end product of that effort. I had insisted that a single irrigation canal was more important than a hundred clinics, and I stayed close to the work site for some seven years directing the project. I sacrificed everything for it. I am not exaggerating when I say that I poured the decades of experience I had accumulated in Afghanistan—and in fact, everything that I had learned and experienced since I was a child—into this project. And at that moment in 2009, I was about to see the fruits of those labors before me.

My Ties to Afghanistan

My first connection to Afghanistan was through insects and mountains. The chance came to me in June 1978, when I joined the Hindu Kush expedition put together by the Fukuoka Tokōkai, a local mountaineering club from the city of Fukuoka in western Japan. The Hindu Kush range is a large massif linked to the Himalaya-Karakoram ranges. The highest peak in the Hindu Kush is Tirich Mir (7,708 meters), which is regarded as the westernmost part of the "Roof of the World." Most of Afghanistan lies entirely within this great mountain range. (The Marwarid Canal that we dug runs along the southern foothills of the Keshmand Mountains, a branch of this chain.)

The Pamir plateau surrounds the northern base of the Hindu Kush range, a location known for being the home of the cabbage white butterfly (*Pieris rapae*). This high mountainous region is also famous as the habitat of various insects going back to the Ice Age, in particular the *Parnassius apollo* species of swallowtail butterfly. When I was around ten years old, I became enthralled with these insects, and remained so for years; as a result, the Hindu Kush was a place that I wanted to visit at least once. At that point I certainly had no interest in matters like international medical assistance.

I was called back to these mountains after a series of encounters that I will talk about later. Ever since that time, I seem to be always traveling around the vast foothills of the Hindu Kush. However, the amazing, invisible bonds of fate are even more far-reaching. Had I not been interested in insects, I probably would have no connection to Afghanistan. Had I not met the small-town postmaster who took me with him as he traveled around the mountains near our hometown . . . had I not met the members of the mountaineering club . . . had I not met a German physician who was putting her heart into a Hansen's disease clinic . . . had I not met so many Japanese workers, including the staff at our offices, whose fates have been tied to mine for close to thirty years . . . had I not provided medical treatment at refugee camps . . . if my family had been different people . . . That series of encounters and occurrences is like the countless folds of the Hindu Kush mountains. When I look at the snow-capped mountains, the thirty-some years seem like a dream and I feel a curious, deep emotion welling up within me.

Afghanistan: Its People and Natural Environment

Afghanistan is a mountainous country that encompasses the better part of the Hindu Kush range. It covers an area slightly larger than France and extends from latitude 29º N to 38º N. It lies in the middle of the Eurasian landmass and is completely landlocked. To the north lie Turkmenistan, Uzbekistan, and Tajikistan, which were formerly part of the Soviet Union. Iran is to the west, while the country's eastern and southern areas share a 2,650-kilometer border with Pakistan. The northeastern part of the country also just barely touches China at the eastern tip of the Wakhan Corridor.

Afghanistan has a dry climate due to the string of arid zones that lie across Central Asia, and the differences between hot and cold are acute. It has a rainy season due to the winter monsoons generated from the Indian Ocean, and wet snow falls on the highlands. However, the cumulative precipitation is small compared to that in the Himalayas to the east, with the annual volume of 327 millimeters per year amounting to a third of the world average. There are four seasons, though the temperatures vary depending on the elevation.

Estimates of the population at the time of writing range from 20 million to 24 million; the precise figure is unknown. Farmers are generally said to account for more than 80 percent of the total and nomadic peoples about 10 percent; a few percent are engaged in forestry in the mountains. The large

Afghanistan and Its Neighbors

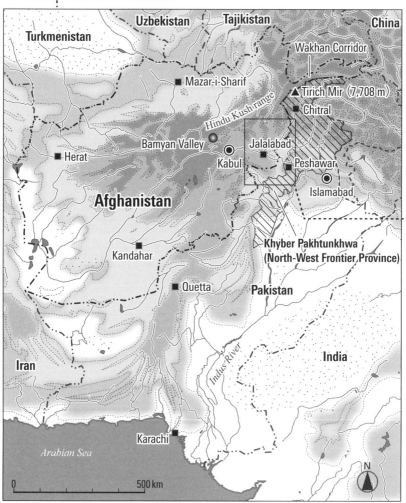

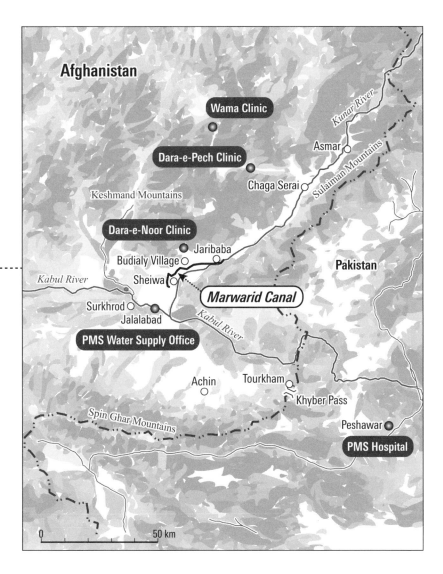

capital city of Kabul is a special case, but on the whole, Afghanistan can be described as an agrarian country. The rugged mountainous regions have kept invaders at bay, and it is common for people to lead self-sufficient lives deep in the mountains.

The Wisdom of Coexistence

As centuries-old references to it as "a crossroads of peoples" suggest, another distinctive feature of Afghanistan is its complex ethnic makeup. This is so varied that practically each one of the countless deep valleys created by the enormous Hindu Kush massif contains a different ethnic group or tribe. Afghanistan's largest ethnic group is the Pashtuns with approximately 8 million people, followed by the Tajiks, the Hazaras, the Uzbeks, and the Turkmens. Add in the smaller ethnic groups and the result is a mosaic nation formed out of a jumble of more than twenty peoples and their respective languages. Given such circumstances, those living here since antiquity have developed the wisdom of coexisting with different groups. This, along with the Islamic religion that binds them together, can be called the tradition that has rooted itself deep in their hearts over the millennia.

If the composition of ethnic groups in Afghanistan is complex, the tribal structure is even more so. Regional and blood ties are strong in Afghan society, particularly in the rural villages. Rather than political ideologies or economic trends, it is those bonds that frequently determine political actions. Constrained by geographical conditions, each region has quite a strong sense of local autonomy and control, and ties with the center are weak. Village communities are ruled mainly by the local *jirga*, an autonomous assembly of community elders. This is a society where there is generally no distinction between being a soldier and being a farmer; the men who farm are also the men-at-arms who defend their village. In the early days of the Soviet-Afghan War (1979–1989), those assorted farmers formed the backbone of the fight against the government army and the Soviet forces that supported it.

Here let me touch on a point that foreigners find difficult to understand. When a foreign army occupies an area, people who collaborate with it will certainly appear, and will stand alongside the occupiers to put down opposing forces. However, after some time passes, the foreign forces come to realize that they are being used. Those collaborators have regional and blood ties that go beyond the difference between friend or foe. There are many instances where, before you realize it, the people you are collaborating with all turn out to be related to one another, or they may have some secret understandings

Major Ethnic Groups

The author receives a warm welcome from villagers in a mountainous region of Afghanistan.

with one another, and you become trapped in their web of relationships.

More than a few of my acquaintances became mercenaries for foreign armies. However, knowing that they had relatives among the enemy troops, they would deliberately shoot off target and engage in showy "gunfights" that impressed their employers and embedded correspondents to no end. They would shrewdly accept high pay and rifles, snipe at the "friendly" foreign forces on their way home, and then happily chat with their relatives from the "enemy" forces as they shared their battle reports for the day. Such stories were not at all unusual. It is normal for foreign armies to be uncertain who is their enemy or their friend and to become gnawed by suspicion and doubt. In recent years, there has been a dramatic rise in the number of incidents in which a foreign army has been fired on by the government forces they had been training.

This pattern is not restricted to armies; foreign aid organizations are also affected by it. In a society that might best be thought of as one where the fix is in on a grand scale, placing respect for regional and blood ties above everything else is a way to survive being tossed about in an ocean of territorial conflicts.

One US army commander who had a difficult time putting down armed insurgents later reminisced that the enemy normally showed themselves to be genial peasants, but when the chance came, they would turn into ferocious assailants. This observation is correct.

Pashtunwali

When we talk about a "country," we imagine a modern state with a central government and an administrative structure that extends throughout the country's territory, along with a set of laws governing people's activities. It would be difficult to say that Afghanistan is that sort of modern state governed by the rule of law. However, it also would be overly hasty to conclude, based on this, that it is a failed nation in a state of anarchy. Even though the sense of local autonomy may be quite strong, and even though tribes and peoples are in a jumble and fight among themselves, they have a shared unwritten law that provides cohesiveness to the world that is Afghanistan. Here, when you ask someone where they come from, they nearly always respond, "From Afghanistan." Invariably, the first stage of your conversation is, "Of course you are, but from which province of Afghanistan?" To be sure, there is conflict among peoples and tribes and there is a discriminatory hierarchy, but there is scant soil to nurture the sort of fanatical ethnic nationalism that would cause the country to fragment like the former Yugoslavia.

The famous unwritten law of Afghanistan is called Pashtunwali (the codes of the Pashtun), and while there are some differences depending on region and ethnic group, it can be thought of as a set of common codes that governs rural Afghan society. Even though their influence over the Westernizing urban classes is weakening, these codes remain as strong as ever among most of the farm villages in the country's eastern regions.

Typical examples of such codes are those of *melmestia* (hospitality) and *badal* (vengeance). These codes in the farming regions are stronger than foreigners would imagine. *Melmestia* is the custom of being hospitable when someone—even a stranger—is recognized as being a friendly guest and not a person whom you would lift a hand against. Even if a person is an enemy of your blood relatives and there has been some dispute that has lasted generations, you absolutely do not attack them when they are your guest. For example, from an international perspective, the prevalent understanding was that Al Qaeda and the Taliban were partners, and Al Qaeda's leader, Osama bin Laden, was in league with the Taliban. In fact, however, at least during the years of Taliban rule, a more accurate interpretation of the relationship was that Al Qaeda was a guest of the Taliban, and the unwritten law that "a guest is someone you do not betray without reason" was a persuasive one for the general population. As another example of *melmestia*, when I traveled around work sites in the hinterlands I often encountered strict checkpoints run by the US army. Other than those cases in which foreign forces were directly involved, when my local driver would say, "This is a foreign guest" to the Afghan soldier handling interpretation, that soldier would pass us through with no more than an "OK, you can go" gesture. If my driver and the soldier were from the same place, they wouldn't even bother with the gesture. I used to be able to travel anywhere thanks to that. This is a matter of respecting the other party's culture and customs.

Badal is revenge: "An eye for an eye and a tooth for a tooth." The word *dushman* (enemy) has particular echoes here; it, too, refers to a customary concept that can be difficult for foreigners to understand. The *dushman* may be someone connected with a generations-old conflict between families, or he may just be someone who has treated you unfairly, but in either case *badal* is considered a justifiable response. Even among the Afghan workers at PMS, it was not unusual to have someone suddenly take time off for "family reasons" in order to deal with such "enemies."

Understandably, there are ways to get around this. A resolution to a conflict may be imposed by the elders of a region when an entire village is inconvenienced by some unproductive conflict. In some cases, the conflict may be resolved if one party sues for peace by offering money or sheep to the other party. Conversely, in the case of treatment that is unreasonable in anyone's view, the act of *badal* is commended. For example, if some unscrupulous, powerful individual killed a weaker person and that person had no adult male sons or relatives, that person's mother would raise a child to be the one who wreaked vengeance. There have been cases in which someone has been invited to a banquet and then poisoned. If the act of *badal* is accomplished years after the original offense, people will praise it as "glorious" to have achieved this "happy" dream. Local newspapers will not infrequently have articles with titles like "Murder Committed by Youth"; most of these are about cases of *badal*. People tend to regard the killings as admirable, or at least understandable. In any event, given that the popular story of the Forty-Seven Loyal Retainers is seen in Japan as a tale of admirable behavior, the concept of honorable killing to avenge wrongdoing is not something that is completely foreign to the Japanese.

These killings for revenge are different from the murders within the family that we see these days in Japan. I heard an Afghan journalist who visited Japan say he was greatly surprised at news stories about murders of parents and violence toward children. The journalist said that this was the first time he had heard of such things, and he concluded that crime in Japan was terrible. It is ironic that these incidents are far more numerous in Japan, an advanced country where the idea of human rights has supposedly taken root, than in Afghanistan. Could it be that ethical sensibilities decline in proportion to the rise in consciousness of personal rights?

When you associate with people in Afghanistan for a long time, you simply cannot choose only the things that you like. Every coin has a good side and a bad side. In fact, there are many cases in which the measure by which you decide whether something is good or not is colored by your personal circumstances and preferences. I think that to coexist means having fundamental relationships with people whose likes and dislikes, views of beauty and ugliness, and concepts of good and evil are contrary to your own.

Memories of Encounters

1946–1985

Chapter 1

Heaven Is with Us

Truth, as the saying goes, is stranger than fiction. I had no ties or connections with Afghanistan or Pakistan—yet the fact that I became close to that region almost as though I had been drawn to it is certainly no mere coincidence. At the same time, it is not, as people frequently misunderstand, that I had some firm beliefs or lofty ideas that drew me there. When I reminisce on the developments that led to my taking on the job that I did, I cannot help but think about all the encounters I had—with people, with events, with the times themselves—encounters that played a role quite apart from my conscious feelings and intentions.

Recounting the developments that led to my starting this job would turn this into a mere autobiography. Still, the way I have remembered events and interpreted them is somewhat autobiographical, so I will just put together the bits and pieces of facts as I saw them in that vein.

Childhood Recollections

I was born on September 15, 1946—just thirteen months after Japan's defeat in World War II—in the Mikasa district of Fukuoka, one of the cities bombed to ruins during the war. Two years later, we moved to the city of Wakamatsu (now part of Kitakyūshū), my parents' hometown. Accordingly, my earliest recollections are of living in Wakamatsu.

The family of my father, Nakamura Tsutomu (born in 1903), was almost completely wiped out in the great Fukuoka air raid of June 1945. So our main ties were with my mother Hideko's relatives, the Tamais, in Wakamatsu. Before the war, the Tamai family had been a not-insignificant presence around Dōkai Bay, where Wakamatsu Port is located, owing to their creation of a dockworkers' association handling coal called the Tamai Company during my grandfather Kingorō's time. But when I knew my grandfather, he was already advanced in age and had lost his former vigor; my only remaining impression of him is that of a genial old man. Due to circumstances I knew nothing of as a child, he had moved out of the family's main house, where we were living. I thus became more closely acquainted with his spouse, my grandmother Man.

This was an era when coal still reigned as the leading source of energy for industry. Wakamatsu stood in the lower reaches of the Onga River, where the Chikuhō coalfields were clustered. Thanks to its role as a port town for shipping coal, Wakamatsu was part of the vital and bustling Kitakyūshū Industrial Zone, alongside the nearby Yawata Steel Works. The Tamai family, too, still had echoes of its prewar heyday. The bonds among my relatives were strong, and I remember that during the postwar years, when food was scarce, family members were coming in and out of the main house like it was their own home.

The author Hino Ashihei—this was actually the pen name of my uncle, Tamai Katsunori, Kingorō's oldest son—depicted the fortunes of the Tamai family and its business in his novel *Hana to ryū* (Flowers and dragons). That book, which was published in 1953, was a sensation, and it has been made into a movie several times. Some of those films portrayed events in the style of a gangster story, and the Tamai family and its relations were sometimes mistaken for members of a yakuza gang. Many quite interesting things did happen in the family's ambit, but I have no bad memories in that regard. I should note that the Tamai Company was no longer in existence when I was living in Wakamatsu; it had been absorbed into the Industrial Patriotic Society during the war years. Our relatives eked out an existence doing the kinds of jobs found around a port town, such as running a water-supply company, raising sunken ships, and the like.

It was the pen of Hino Ashihei that bound the Tamai family together. During the war years, my uncle had won the prestigious Akutagawa Prize for his novel *Funnyōtan* (Tales of excrement and urine). While he was in the service he wrote a trilogy of war novels that became amazingly popular, including the noted *Mugi to heitai* (translated as *Wheat and Soldiers*), and he became a national hero. After Japan's defeat, he was denounced as a war collaborator, and for a while he was banned from writing for publication. However, his passion for literature remained, and subsequently he took up his pen again. But he continued to question the meaning of the war, and he suddenly took his own life after completing his novel *Kakumei zengo* (Before and after the revolution), which depicted the years of postwar chaos. This was in January 1960, more than fourteen years after the war ended.

The most vivid memories I have from life in Wakamatsu are of the presence of my grandmother Man, who was a fiery "war mother" sort, and of how my uncle the writer lived his life. Man had been born to an old Hiroshima country samurai family, and she showed this background in her demeanor

The author's grandparents, Tamai Kingorō (right) and Tamai Man (left). Man's mother is at center.

Group photo of Tamai Company employees. (Both photos on this page courtesy of the Tamai family.)

as a strict disciplinarian. During the war, when the bombing of Wakamatsu started, everyone else in the family evacuated, but she stayed behind. According to family legend, she used a bamboo spear to knock away the incendiaries and keep the house from burning down. When I was young, she would sit ensconced next to an oblong brazier in a room by the entrance to the house and smoke tobacco in an old-fashioned Japanese *kiseru* pipe. This image was like a symbol of the family's solidity, inspiring awe and giving us all a sense of security. My grandmother's admonitions took root and remained with me as my own ethical perspective: Take the lead in protecting the weak; regard all legitimate trades as equally honorable; respect the lives of even the smallest of creatures—these are some of the lessons I learned from her that I have been following ever since.

The Conversion of Hino Ashihei

In his writings, my uncle Hino Ashihei often castigated himself as "simple-minded" and a "fool." With wartime experiences that took him around China, to the Philippines, and to Burma (Myanmar), he likely had the longest record when it came to covering the ordinary soldier on the front lines. He was there at the army's direction to serve as a member of the information corps, and it cannot be denied that what he produced was published to be read as a tool to whip up the nation's fighting spirit. After the war, both left-wing activists and the US occupation forces condemned him for this as a war collaborator. I do wonder what his state of mind was like in those years.

My uncle seems to have been pleased with his houses. He gave them names, calling his place in Wakamatsu "Kahakudō" (the cave of the water sprite) and the one in Tokyo "Donkoan" (the *donko*'s hermitage). The *donko* is a small fish that in those days you could see everywhere in the shallows around a river's mouth. "These fish flee quickly as a school when someone casts a shadow over them; they're timid and ungainly," wrote Hino. "Everybody says, 'Oh, they're just *donko*,' and ignores them. . . . But I can't help identifying with them in their dimwitted condition."

As I see it, Hino was a child of an age in which he was constrained by the dramatic transformations that took place during and after the war. In particular, it is beyond doubt that, for someone who had dedicated the culmination of his youthful years to the war, Japan's defeat was a cruel experience. August 15, 1945—the day Japan surrendered—marked the dividing point. Until just the day before, the Japanese people had all been chanting, "Destroy America and Britain!" But suddenly they were transformed. Former army officers began to operate dance halls for American soldiers. Men who taken the lead in acts of barbarism on the battlefield acted as though they had been victims, pinning the blame for their crimes on the military authorities. A general tendency to be unprincipled and insincere prevailed. But as Hino confronted the past, even if in his head he could reject the acts of war that had taken place, he could not easily make a clean break with the emotions the war had left in his heart. The new postwar world moved forward in a way that swept away even his private thoughts in its muddy currents. He must certainly have had a sense of deep shame within his heart.

Hino put on a show of having inner strength, of being an optimist who could make you laugh with his unique sense of humor, and of being something of a decadent with a weakness for alcohol, but he was undeniably tormented by the struggle between his delicate poet's soul and the shadow of war. There are all manner of arguments about Hino's ideological conversion and his suicide. However, having dedicated his life to the war cause, he could not nimbly change course. It took him a decade to get to the point where he rejected the war. He mocked himself for the sluggish pace of his conversion, saying he was displaying "the dimwittedness of a *donko*," though I don't believe that a decade is such a long time. He praised the beauty of human sentiment with its never-ending love, and he tried to discover whatever sparks of beauty there might be even in weakness and ugliness. Despite the fact that there was no shortage of people who shared his feelings and listened to what he had to say, he tragically decided to end his own life. If my uncle were alive now, he would probably have things to say about the shameless ways of today's world, where people change so easily.

The works of Hino Ashihei were among the first books that I laid my hands on when I was young. My father was part of the local Kyushu Literary Circle, so he had complimentary copies of all of my uncle's books lining his shelves. Accordingly, I embraced Hino more as a writer with whom I identified rather than as a relative. The verse of his that is carved into the monument at the peak of Mount Takatō overlooking Wakamatsu Harbor is a penetrating one. I am not a soldier, but when I consider the transcending beauty that survived the turmoil and bloodshed he encountered in the war, even as he was smeared by the ugliness of the human world, I cannot help but feel deep emotions.

> The scent of a single chrysanthemum
> decorating a muddied rucksack
> as the blue of the sky shines into the eyes
> of the soldier walking the streets of a foreign land.

Tamai Man and Hino Ashihei. (Photo courtesy of the Tamai family.)

Only the first two lines of the verse are carved into the monument, but without the second two, the meaning of the poem is cut in half. The second part of the poem expresses the sadness and homesickness of a Japanese soldier sent to another country. Most Japanese in those days were farmers, and hazy skies and barley fields were part of the spring landscape. The vast skies and fields of grain found in the place the army reached on its march surely would have vividly brought to mind the soldier's hometown.

The Boundless World of Small Insects

I lived in Wakamatsu through my first year of elementary school. Then, in 1952, we moved to the town (now city) of Koga in Fukuoka. I did not know the reason for the move, but it seems to have been a matter of debts accumulating due to the failure of my father's business and the reckless ease with which he cosigned other people's loans. We were reduced to poverty, and we moved to the last house the Tamai family owned. Our home and all of our possessions were mortgaged, and an endless stream of people kept coming to collect debts. At the time, banks did not handle dunning in a gentlemanly fashion. Evil-looking men suddenly pushed their way into the house and wrote down prices in chalk on everything from dressers and antiques to paltry items like a child's desk. I now realize that this meant our property was "under attachment."

When this sort of thing happens time after time, it would be natural for the mind of a child to grow uneasy. However, I don't think anyone around me was brooding. After the war, because every household had sunk to the depths of poverty, children did not think matters were that grave. My hard-drinking parents did not seem all that worried, and even if the money was drying up, the drinking parties did not come to an end. Relatives and acquaintances would nonchalantly come uninvited to dinner, and we would do likewise (it was normal to turn up unannounced at the houses of relatives when you were down and out). There was a point where you just thought it would work out somehow. And indeed, things did work out. My parents lived long lives, and now I am leisurely writing up my memories of the past. Something like this underlying optimism in the face of financial troubles can be seen in today's Afghanistan.

The most decisive encounter I had in Koga was when I was in third grade. It was with Kikkawa-san, the local postmaster, whose son was one of my classmates. He was a butterfly collector who often took walks through the hills and fields in the area, and he started inviting me to come along.

I think it was summer vacation when he showed me an amazingly beautiful insect mounted with a setting pin. It was about a centimeter and a half long, with a deep-blue and red pattern that shone with a metallic luster, and it looked tough. I asked him, "Is this from Japan?"

"Yes," he replied, "They're everywhere. Next time, I'll take you to the mountains around here and catch one for you." Several days later, just as we were leaving the area of human habitation and starting on a mountain trail, a small locust-like insect flew across my path and came to a landing several meters down the way. As I drew close, it again flew off in the same direction I was headed. "That's the same insect I showed you the other day," said Kikkawa-san. "It's called a tiger beetle." He captured it with an insect net and showed it to me. Dubious, I looked at the creature that he held pinched between his fingers; there, trying to escape, was undeniably the same beautiful insect in question. He said, "You try holding it," but when I haphazardly tried to do so, it bit me with its sharp mandibles. I released my grip, and it was gone in an instant.

As I brought my injured fingertips up to my face, I caught a smell like that of a just-sharpened new pencil. It seems that when you capture a tiger beetle it releases this scent. Kikkawa-san also taught me that the reason the tiger beetle is also known colloquially in Japanese as the *michi-oshie* (trail guide) is because it really does travel ahead along the path you are taking, as if to say, "Follow me."

Though Kikkawa-san probably did not realize it, for me this was a decisive event. The insect world taught me that people can see only what they try to see. After that, whenever I had a day off from school, I always set out for the mountains, and before I knew it I had become a junior insect watcher. I turned down a daily allowance of ten yen and instead got fifty yen every Sunday. In those days, it cost thirty yen for a round-trip ticket from Koga Station to the Komono bus stop at the foot of the mountain known as Nishiyama. With the remaining twenty yen, I could buy some bread and a bottle of milk. I would wake up at five, make some rice balls, fill my water bottle with tea, and set off feeling like I was on an expedition. Those days off were so much fun. When Kikkawa-san brought me along, on top of paying my bus fare he would also explain things. The outings with him were the most wonderful nature school I ever attended. He knew a lot not only about insects in general, but about other plants and animals, minerals, geography, and climate as well. He could field nearly all of my questions. You would expect a small-town postmaster to be busy. I have no idea how he became so learned.

The lives of the iridescent beetles that swarm around cow manure; the insect feasts around the chestnut oaks; the places where the ground beetles hibernate over the winter; the insects that live in the water: the world of insects is infinitely great. I read the translation of Jean-Henri Fabre's *Souvenirs Entomologiques* around that time, and I became more and more absorbed in a new universe. Also, my legs and back became toughened from walking in the mountains so often, and eventually I could take hikes without any fatigue. My parents, who had worried about my poor health when we were living in Wakamatsu, were delighted to see me become so vigorous thanks to my engagement with the insect world. But nobody knew that this interest had established my fate to go on to work in Peshawar two decades later.

The author (the youth with the white cap) in his younger days, when he was obsessed with insect collecting.

Family photo. The author is fourth from the right in the front row. (Both photos on this page courtesy of the Tamai family.)

The Road to Becoming a Physician

I had completely adopted the affectations of an insect watcher, and my dream was to learn from Fabre, live in the countryside, and observe and study insects. Around that time, the publisher Hoikusha came out with a landmark illustrated book called *Genshoku konchū daizukan: Chōga-hen (A grand illustrated color guide to insects: Butterflies and moths)*, and I read it assiduously from cover to cover. The author, Shirōzu Takashi, was a professor at Kyushu University. That made me want to study entomology at the university's School of Agriculture.

However, my father was a strict person. I knew for certain that he would say, "Going to university because of your hobby is ridiculous." In those days, probably one-third of my classmates had gone to work once they finished junior high school. It would be safe to say that going on to university was something special. And back then, unlike today, whatever your parents said was final.

Around this time, I had another encounter that provided me with the basis for a compromise with my father. That was my encounter with Christianity—or, more precisely, with a work by the Meiji-era Japanese Christian pioneer Uchimura Kanzō. I had attended junior high at a mission school called Seinan Gakuin, so naturally I had already come face to face with Christianity. Up to then, the core of my ethical views had been formed by the authoritative code of my father Tsutomu and my grandmother Man. Aside from the external trappings of a creed, both of them, it would be safe to say, were governed by a Confucian/Japanese ethical perspective that above all strictly forbade any sort of crookedness. While I wouldn't go so far as to say that *The Analects of Confucius* was my favorite book, it resonated deeply with me as something that explained the rules a person should follow as a matter of course.

I will forego the details of the developments that followed, but I should note that Uchimura's *Kōsei e no saidai ibutsu* (published in English as *The Greatest Legacy*) had a comparably strong impact on me. Like sensitive youth of preceding generations, I, too, found that something of an archaic sense of mission lived within in me on the order of wanting to devote my future to my country. At the time, people everywhere in Japan had long been faced with the grave social issue of inadequate medical care. Accordingly, I was determined to go to medical school. My father was in complete agreement with this, and gave me permission to go to university.

Generally speaking, however, human motivations are complex. A clear and readily understood explanation is artificial in some way. My actual feelings were wavering between a sense of mission and a desire to pursue my personal interests, and my decision to go to medical school was rather tentative. Indeed, it would be wrong to say that I plowed into the study of medicine burning with some high-minded spirit. I remember that I had in mind the calculating rationalization that, while I could transfer from the Faculty of Medicine to the Faculty of Agriculture, the reverse would not be possible—and that starting out with medical studies was the ideal way of getting the agreement of my stubborn father.

In any case, it is certain that, had I gone on to study entomology at this time as I had personally wanted, I would have neither taken up my Peshawar job nor been active in Afghanistan. My encounter with Christianity was what made those things possible. In particular, I read the Sermon on the Mount passage in the Gospel of Matthew so many times that I learned it by heart. When I think about the relationship between humans and nature, the vivid impression I received remains unchanged today. Jesus declares, "Consider the lilies of the field, . . . Even Solomon in all his glory was not arrayed like one of these" (Matt. 6:28–29, King James version). As I read it, this means: "You have been provided with the things that you need. Don't seek warm clothes or rich foods. Just seek the Way. Heaven will be with you." That may be a Japanese-flavored interpretation, but theological debates are of no concern here. For myself, based on those words, I simply tried to find a universal way to be a human being.

Immanuel

The Japanese title of this book, *Ten, tomo ni ari* (lit. "heaven is with us") corresponds to the Hebrew name "Immanuel." This is the essence of what the Bible expresses. If you set aside the nonessentials, everything is summarized in that phrase. It connects to everything, like something that runs underground.

To backtrack a bit, I have an indelible memory of something else that happened to me as a child. When I was about six years old, I fell into a coma from some major illness. On the day it happened, I had gone with my mother to pay a call on my ailing grandfather in his home. He tended to be lying down because he had had a stroke. Even so, he was a cheerful host, as always. "Have a beer before you go!" he said to my mother. (He didn't drink alcohol himself, but he knew she would be happy to have some.) But in his confused state, he brought her a bottle of soy sauce instead. The two of them had a big laugh about it. Then, on our way home, my mother let me have some ice cream, which was a rare treat. My memory of what happened next is gone.

Several weeks passed that I know nothing about. When I came to, it was evening. Just a little bit of outside light poked through the window of the gloomy sickroom. As it did, the lead character from a comic strip running in the newspapers at the time sneaked in through the window and, laughing, tried to jab a long nail into my chest. I shrieked and cried out in panic, but the adults watching over me laughed and paid no attention. Shortly thereafter, someone who must have been the doctor in charge came in. "He's hallucinating," he said, and I was taken to the emergency room. People wearing white hospital gowns pressed in on me. They called out, "Ringer's! Ringer's!" and when that saline solution was brought forth they used a surprisingly large syringe to poke me in the rear. With that, I lost consciousness again.

At the time, I did not know what either "Ringer's" or "hallucination" meant. Thinking about it later, I believe I had contracted some serious illness and slipped into a state of shock. The people around me thought I was near death. Then my grandfather had another stroke, and they wondered whether he or I would be the first to go.

By the time I was released from the hospital, my grandfather was no longer with us. The funeral had already taken place, and I was told he had passed on to the next world. But this was something my six-year-old mind could not come to terms with. These memories of my first experience with death left a long trail. I thought about what this world was, and about where people go when they die. I lost some of my childish innocence, and I developed a special attachment to old things that were withering away.

Around that time, the illustrations for a certain fairy tale began to haunt me. The story went something like this.

> Once upon a time, there was a young horse. He prayed fervently to God that he would become a strong, fast horse, able to travel through the desert for days without complaint. In response to this great zeal, a servant of God appeared and spoke to him. "I will grant your desire. However, I do not know what form your body will take as a result."
>
> The horse accepted those words. His prayers were answered, and he became a strong horse, one that was fast and did not tire. He was beside himself with joy. However, his delight did not last long. One day, when he visited a spring to drink some water, he was surprised by what he saw. Reflected in the water's surface was an ill-favored form that didn't looked like a horse at all, with a crimped mane and a long neck that resembled an elephant's trunk. He had been turned into a camel.

This was probably a Middle Eastern folk tale. In any case, the illustrations that went with the story showed the horse looking up from the bottom left corner of a two-page spread to an elderly person who was meant to be God at the top right corner of the opposite page. The white-bearded old man had a gentle face but an admonitory expression.

After that, this image would come to my mind vividly, just like a hallucination, and I would converse with it. For all that, I was a normal, unsophisticated child. Sometimes I lied, and sometimes I got into mischief. However, if I saw something beautiful, that old man would appear and smile. If I did something bad, he would scold me, and if I did something good, he would offer praise. Eventually the image of that old man came to resemble my grandparents, and I had the sense that they were always within me. This sense remained with me through my junior high school years. Though it gradually faded after that, it resonated with the words "Heaven is with us" and touched my heart.

I am not talking about some sort of divine possession. In psychiatric terms, what I was seeing could be explained as the image of the superego. But for me, it is not something that requires a logical explanation. I see it as a thing you experience when you are at the point of life or death. I think you discover there is a sacred space that really exists in the depths where all human words and actions fail, where there is the "way of humanity" that runs through everyone, regardless of their different cultures, regions, and eras. In the six decades since then, while I certainly cannot claim that I have been following God's will, I have at least been consistently trying to be faithful.

The US Military: War and Peace

When I matriculated in the Kyushu University Faculty of Medicine in 1968, I met with an unexpected turn of events. Public opinion was divided at the time regarding the US-Japan Security Treaty of 1960, and with its ten-year renewal then coming up, the fires were rekindled and major actions had begun on campuses around Japan. The catalyzing events were the arrival of a US nuclear aircraft carrier at Sasebo in Nagasaki Prefecture and the crash of a US Air Force F4 Phantom jet on the Kyushu University campus. As a member of the university's student council, inevitably I was wrapped up in developments.

In 1968, the Vietnam War had turned into a quagmire, and US aircraft making sorties from Okinawa were conducting fierce air raids on Vietnam. In the face of Japanese public opinion and the peace movements whose members strongly opposed nuclear weapons, the US government expressed the view that the Japanese must get rid of their aversion to nuclear defense, and the American forces went out of their way to dock the nuclear aircraft carrier *Enterprise* at Sasebo in Nagasaki. In response, a vigorous opposition movement arose around the country, with the people of Sasebo in the lead. Peace groups, labor unions, and university students turned out in full force in Sasebo and launched protests. The building housing what was then the General Education Department at Kyushu University was turned into a base for sending people to the demonstrations, and numerous student activists congregated there.

At the time, people who had survived the battlefields of World War II formed a core element in Japanese society. In addition, memories of the air raids around Kyushu and especially of the atomic bombing of Nagasaki remained fresh. Nearly everyone was furiously and wholeheartedly opposed to the *Enterprise* coming to port. I was, too, and I supported the aggressive use of force.

However, some student activists lapsed into overheated affectations. They deluded themselves into thinking that they were "revolutionaries" who had "won the support of the masses." As the theoretical disputes and factional strife heated up, I became uncomfortable and resigned from my position. I simply could not accept this political aspect that had become so removed from the people's pleas for peace. And when I later saw the students who had been shouting "Smash the system!" easily transform themselves and, after graduating, shrewdly take jobs in the medical establishment or at major companies, memories of my uncle Hino Ashihei, who had spent more than a decade struggling with the issues of war and peace before taking his own life, would come back to me. Deep down, I could not be so calm.

Two decades later I would once again come into contact with the US military in a different time and place—namely, in Afghanistan. Whether I liked it or not, matters of war and peace were problems that I could not avoid due to the presence of those US forces.

Chapter 2

The Road to Peshawar

The Point of Living: My Years as a Psychiatrist

In 1973, upon my graduation from the Kyushu University Faculty of Medicine, I joined the staff of the national Hizen Psychiatric Center in Saga Prefecture to work in the field of neuropsychiatry. My motivations for choosing this field were rather casual. One was that, at the time, I was interested in human mental phenomena. Also, I thought that psychiatry would leave me free time to go insect collecting and hiking through the mountains. In addition, one of the thinkers that I particularly admired—alongside Uchimura Kanzō, Miyazawa Kenji, Nishida Kitarō, and Karl Barth—was the psychiatrist Viktor Frankl.

However, I did not find psychiatry an easy profession. It is difficult to face people who are suffering psychologically, and my interactions with patients forced me to think about many things. One of the most important jobs in psychiatry is to discover and prevent plans to commit suicide. Once, after I stopped a patient with schizophrenia under my care from attempting suicide, that patient posed a question to me:

"I have no sense of meaning in my life. Doctor, how about you? What do you live for?" I was at a loss for words. "My job and my interest in insects" would not be a serious answer, and I was not so religious that I could expound on the significance of "the life that has been given to us." In the final analysis, I was not adhering consistently to any firm convictions in my own life; I was merely being carried along by the flow of duty and human sentiment as shaped by the circumstances of the moment.

What I realized then was that the reality of being myself, or an individual, is a shaky thing. In physical terms, I exist as a *Homo sapiens*, but in the mental sphere it is exceedingly hard to get a grip on "myself" and "the ego." Still, I felt that I had grasped the difficult concept that humans are relationships. The psychiatrist-philosopher Karl Jaspers expressed it clearly. As he put it, the self-realizing person does not exist, and the human who only regards himself will cease to exist. We realize ourselves in our relationships with others.

I do not know much beyond that about the details of Jaspers' thinking. But as a clinician, I also took note of Frankl's warning about the trap posed by psychoanalysis. His perspective might be summarized as follows: Meaning is hidden from humans. When a human tries to will that hidden meaning into existence, it becomes an artifact of human behavior and therefore a fabrication. This causes the person to fall into despair. The person who is suffering does not need to become aware of the unconscious through an analysis of cause and effect, but rather to restore their consciousness to the rich world of the unconscious.

At the time, I found these arguments persuasive. When the biblical author writes, "Vanity of vanities; all is vanity" (Ecclesiastes), and when the Buddhist chants, "Form is exactly emptiness, and emptiness exactly form" (Heart Sutra), they are saying the same sort of thing. "Emptiness" does not mean "nothing." It is as though there may be some sort of richness and sacredness hidden within.

So why is it that humans can understand some holy thing that is hidden from their consciousness? Frankl has said that the conscience is the organ that senses meaning. Theologian Karl Barth argues for the natural ranking of God and Man and their oneness, and for a universality of grace common to everyone, while rejecting the free, homocentric theology of modern times. The *Analects* of Confucius clearly state, "When you know a thing, to hold that you know it; and when you do not know a thing, to allow that you do not know it—this is knowledge," while also including the message, "You should learn from the past if you want to learn of the future."

Perhaps it's a bit of overthinking, but this was the greatest realization of my days as a psychiatrist. I feel it was a final settling of accounts on the frequently confused thinking of my youth. I think this is why I did not feel any special sense of discomfort when I later came into contact with Islam in Peshawar and Afghanistan. To the contrary, I believe my own ideas were reaffirmed, and I was able to talk with everyone on the same level.

Taking the Job in Peshawar

Moving away from psychiatry, I then worked for four years as a neurologist at a hospital for work-related accident cases in the city of Ōmuta in Fukuoka Prefecture. During that time, I also joined the Fukuoka Tokōkai mountaineering group on an expedition to Tirich Mir. As we pushed our way through the Hindu Kush range, I developed an affection for the area. However, I gave no serious thought to taking up work as a physician there.

In 1978, I wanted to be in the field of neurosurgery. I wound up working as assistant director at a neurosurgical hospital in the town of Hirokawa,

A street scene in Peshawar, where the author began his new job.

A kebab stall in Peshawar's old city.

where one of my university seniors was employed as director, until 1982. He was a unique sort of person, and a bit of a samurai sort. We got along well. He allowed me to do a six-month internship in the anesthesiology department of Kurume University, and I intended to continue working at his hospital.

Then, however, I was approached by a group called the Japan Overseas Christian Medical Cooperative Service (JOCS), and I ended up taking a new job abroad. To prepare for this, I spent six months at Fukuoka Tokushukai Hospital interning in general internal and surgical medicine. The hospital director, Satō Kōzō, was also from Wakamatsu, and he continued to give me his unstinting support for many years thereafter. Compared to the trajectory of my life up to this point, the events that led up to my taking the Peshawar job were surprisingly uncomplicated. It happened that, while on a visit to Japan, Dr. Anwar Ujagar, director of the Mission Hospital Peshawar in Pakistan, had made a request to JOCS for a physician to be sent there. It would be the first time for JOCS to dispatch a physician to an Islamic region in the Middle East, and it seems there was considerable uncertainty within the organization about the matter. When I heard about the request, I thought, "That's someplace where I'd like to work," and announced myself as a candidate. After that, things moved forward without a hitch. Appointments to the post at Mission Hospital Peshawar were for three-year terms; I wound up staying for roughly two terms, totaling around seven years (1984–90).

Starting in 1991, whenever I was back in Japan I would work on a part-time basis at the same neurosurgical hospital in Hirokawa while continuing my activities in Peshawar. I could not have done so without that hospital's support. My return there involved another unforgettable encounter. For certain reasons, I was no longer working for JOCS. Finding myself hard-pressed financially, I visited the hospital director and privately asked if I could have a part-time job. The director of the hospital welcomed me back in good humor, saying I was like a prodigal son to him. That is something I will never forget. I have kept quiet about this exchange up to now, fearing anything I said would come across as a glib remark. However, it seems appropriate that I should record this important behind-the-scenes encounter here.

Peshawar-kai

In September 1983, the Peshawar-kai (Peshawar Society) was created specifically to support the new position I was to take in Peshawar. Officially speaking, the Peshawar-kai is a group that contributes funds to the Peace Japan Medical Services (PMS) foundation, though the relationship goes beyond that.

The author with his family at the Peshawar-kai ceremony held prior to their departure for Pakistan.

The Peshawar-kai office in Fukuoka.

I studied at the Liverpool School of Tropical Medicine that year, and then in 1984, with my family in tow, I took up my new job in Pakistan. The Peshawar-kai was initially made up mainly of my classmates, fellow mountaineers, and people from my church, but gradually it gathered a membership consisting of people who sympathized with our activities in Peshawar and Afghanistan. As the scale of the project expanded, the group was tempered by crises, going through a number of major transformations, and eventually grew from an association of like-minded people into an organization that could support work done on the ground.

As of this writing, we have just three full-time staff members—one in Pakistan and two in Japan—assisted by about two dozen volunteers; this small team collects several hundred million yen in donations every year and handles administrative tasks. Officially, the Peshawar-kai has around 15,000 members, but we have more than 20,000 contributors and publish around 30,000 copies of our quarterly newsletter.

I cannot talk about our work in Peshawar and Afghanistan without acknowledging the kindhearted support we have received from countless people in Japan. I do not—as is often assumed in error—conduct this work all by myself. It is not the slightest exaggeration to say that our three decades of activity are the fruits of goodwill both locally and in Japan. The Peshawar-kai is the primary force in Japan that has continued to support our local efforts both physically and spiritually. Its diverse membership ranges from students, company employees, housewives, teachers, public servants, medical care workers, and engineers to union members and corporate executives. They span the religious and political spectrum as well: we have Buddhist priests and Christian ministers, conservatives and reformers.

In addition to the support of our members, the selfless efforts of the volunteers handling the administrative work are crucial; without them our endeavors on the ground would come to nothing. We can see, from the pleasure they take in their workaday tasks—without trendy talk about "international cooperation"—that each of them is committed to our activities, finding them a source of spiritual sustenance.

In 2009, owing to disturbances in Peshawar, we shifted the center of our operations in the area to Jalalabad in eastern Afghanistan, but we have left the "Peshawar-kai" name unchanged.

The Hansen's Disease Clinic

The opportunity for me to treat Hansen's disease came about in December 1982, when I was on a preliminary visit to the Mission Hospital Peshawar.

I met a German physician named Ruth Pfau, a Catholic nun who had been working at Hansen's disease clinics in Pakistan for some twenty years. Then based at the Marie Adelaide Leprosy Centre in Karachi, she was in the middle of putting together a major program to eradicate Hansen's disease in Pakistan.

Sister Ruth knew that in all of Pakistan the most difficult region was the North-West Frontier Province (today's Khyber Pakhtunkhwa), of which Peshawar was the capital. With the long-extant Hansen's disease ward at the Mission Hospital serving as a treatment center for disease complications, she had worked with the provincial government to set up medicine dispensaries in the province's mountainous region, aiming to dramatically reduce incidences of infection.

However, with around 20,000 Hansen's disease sufferers throughout Pakistan and only three physicians specializing in treating the ailment, she was fighting against the odds by herself. There were 2,400 officially registered patients in the North-West Frontier Province alone, and the actual number looked to be more than five times that. Though Peshawar had a surplus of surgeons and internal medicine physicians, there were no Hansen's disease specialists, and the treatment center was in a horrific plight. Accordingly, when I happened to visit, she entreated me to help if I could.

When I took up my position at the Mission Hospital in May 1984, I went to the director right away and asked to be put in charge of the Hansen's disease ward. Hansen's disease cannot be treated by simply giving someone medicine. The disease attacks peripheral nerves along with the skin. Consequently, the treatments needed are diverse, including reconstructive surgery to deal with motor paralysis, rehabilitation to prevent deformities, measures to deal with plantar ulcers caused by sensory paralysis, measures to prevent loss of eyesight, care for lepra reactions, and other procedures. Treating complications from the disease requires a physician with experience, and I stressed that provision of more adequate treatment for the disease would also be beneficial for the hospital as an institution funded by foreign Christian organizations. After some negotiations, they left it up to me, and we were able to get on track with some real improvements.

For all that, when I started, the operation was more like a charity performance than a hospital ward. It had little substantial equipment and only sixteen sickbeds for 2,400 patients. It really was something more on the order of a field hospital. There was a single trolley that would tip over if you pushed it, a number of bent tweezers, and one stethoscope that would injure your ears if you put it on. We could not disinfect our gauze properly; all we could do was put it in the oven. If it was still white, it was unsterilized; if it was brown, it was sterile. Those were the conditions in which we operated.

The North-West Frontier Province and Adjacent Areas with Many Hansen's Disease Patients

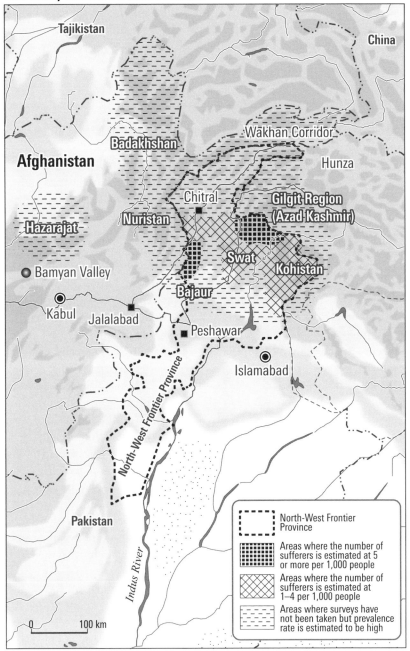

People may say that medical care is not a matter of materials or money, but there are limits to what you can do without resources. As expected, when they came to inspect the ward, the Peshawar-kai officials (the director at the time was Dr. Satō Yūji) were shocked. Their response motivated the efforts to attract donations that continue to the present day.

Improving the Ward

In spite of all the support we received, the first several years were an ongoing struggle. In 1985, we rebuilt one room in the cramped ward to serve as an operating theater, making it possible to do reconstructive surgery. This work involved restoring muscular function to areas where motor paralysis had been caused by the peripheral nerves being attacked. The most common surgeries we performed were for foot drop, wrist drop, and lagophthalmos (an inability to close the eyelid). The operating theater was less than 7 square meters, making for a very cramped space once we put in an operating table. I had to skitter about like a crab, moving sidewise to keep my surgical gown sterile by preventing it from touching the wall. Because power outages were common, I frequently worked by flashlight. It was truly like a field hospital. I did everything, including disinfecting and cleaning the instruments, and carried the patients in and out on my back.

The number of patients rapidly increased, and at times we had to set up tents in the courtyard to accommodate them. We gradually enlarged the ward, but with just me and one nurse looking after more than seventy patients at some points, the work was beyond the limits of our strength. In response to this situation, our relatively healthy patients became our principal source of assistance, taking on various roles at their own initiative. They were sufferers of Hansen's disease themselves, but they happily looked after their fellow patients. They may have come from far away, and had been spending their time listlessly in the ward as though they were in a detention facility. But once they had duties to perform, they worked day and night. They were unpaid volunteers, of course. Some young patients who acquired practical skills became able to work as my medical assistants. They helped with surgery, wrapped casts on limbs, assisted with rehabilitation, and dealt with simple wounds. These volunteers became an important part of our team in the ward.

When I was carrying a patient out of the operating theater on my back after surgery, other patients who still had use of their arms and legs would come rushing, and together they would take charge of transporting the patient. This sort of scene became commonplace. The fact that everyone was taking the initiative to somehow be useful made things cheerful and lively.

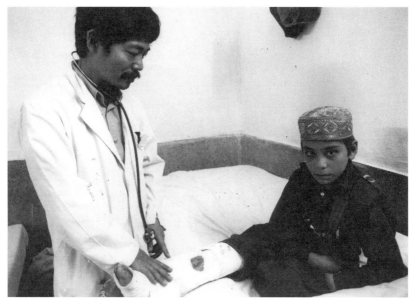

The author treating a child with Hansen's disease.

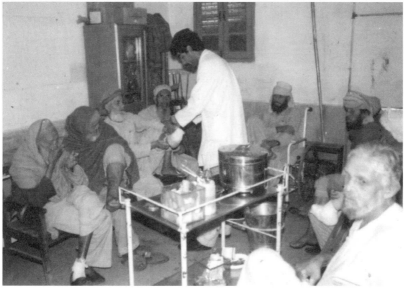

The author's examination room. All of the ward's medical appliances are loaded on the cart in the center of the photo.

Shoemakers at work in the sandal workshop set up in a corner of the ward.

Sandals awaiting free distribution. After the ward started distributing sandals to patients, the number of foot amputations decreased dramatically.

What actually provided the greatest boost, though, was not our obvious accomplishments, like surgery or reconstructive treatment, but rather the fact that we opened a shoe shop in the ward. This requires some explanation. As I mentioned before, Hansen's disease causes sensory paralysis in the arms and legs. Leg disabilities in particular can have devastating consequences in everyday life. Because sufferers do not feel pain, it is easy for them to injure the soles of their feet. When a healthy person gets a pebble in their shoe and develops a blister, they will notice the pain, rest up a bit, and the injury will heal. But when you have sensory paralysis, you do not notice the injury. The wound in that spot remains and eventually a hole develops in the foot. This is a plantar ulcer, and it is a most troublesome thing. If it is left untreated, it can cause skin cancer or osteomyelitis (inflammation of the bone marrow), and in many cases the foot must be amputated.

When I looked at our patients' footwear, I saw that many of the shoes were falling apart and had been mended with nails. It would have been hard to avoid injury when wearing them. Nothing beats prevention, and with that in mind we set up a sandal workshop in a corner of the ward, recruited skilled shoemakers from the town, and distributed their footwear to the patients. The fact is, while shoes that can prevent plantar ulcers from developing were regarded as indispensable in treating Hansen's disease, earlier attempts to provide such footwear to patients in this region had not been successful. People in Peshawar, in the North-West Frontier Province, and in the Afghan countryside have quite a traditional mindset. If you give them something from a foreign country, it will soon turn up for sale, unused, in the bazaar. Accordingly, we made a point of copying sandals of local origin and concentrated on such measures as adding cushioning to the soles to minimize the weight pressing down on areas where injuries can easily occur.

This was a big success. After a large number of sandals from the ward had been distributed, the number of foot amputations performed was dramatically reduced. Now that commercially produced footwear of the same sort has become available in the bazaars, the historic role of the sandal workshop is gradually coming to an end. But an accumulation of small initiatives like this helped support our medical treatment activities.

The Agony of a Patient with Hansen's Disease

One day in 1985, a pair of sisters with their aged mother arrived at the Hansen's disease ward at the Mission Hospital. All three of them were wearing chador that covered their faces, and at first, they approached no one.

After some persuasion and placating on the part of our staff, they timidly produced a wrinkled piece of paper. This turned out to be a registration card that had previously been used at the leprosy center at the Mission Hospital Peshawar. Deciphering the faded ink writing, we discovered they were Afghans who had been registered as new patients there in 1978; their treatment had been interrupted.

In a separate room, our staff had them remove their chador and then involuntarily gasped at what they saw. The younger sister, who was not yet thirty, had a cavity where the bridge of her nose should have been. Her face was deformed, and her fingertips were bent like an eagle's claws. Pustules had ulcerated all over her body, and her skin was hanging in shreds. Her sister, two years her senior, had no hair on her head; their mother had a large burn on her right foot and her skin was necrotizing.

The three were from Kunar, a province in northeastern Afghanistan on the border with Pakistan. They were also victims of war. The internal conflict occasioned by the Soviet invasion broke out in earnest around 1980, and Kunar at the time was one of the sites of fierce battles. Tens of thousands of people became refugees and sought to escape the danger by fleeing to the regions across the border in Pakistan.

Most of these women's male family members had died fighting as mujahideen guerrillas. Protected by several cousins, the women had made it to a refugee camp in Bajaur province, east of the Kunar Valley in Pakistan. They did not even have enough money for the bus fare to Peshawar, and had barely managed to get by with the food distributions at the camp. Of course, they had already used up the year's supply of medicine for Hansen's disease they had received. Their illness had progressed bit by bit. The younger sister, Harima, had boils all over her body, and when she reached a point where she was running a high fever and her pain had grown unbearable, a sympathetic guerrilla leader at the camp brought them to Peshawar.

These women had been frightened by something. It was easy to imagine that they had undergone harsh experiences, but I did not dare to pry. In any case, what people who are ill like this need is to get relief from their illness and to have even just a little bit of their pride as a human being restored to them. The first thing to do was to make them understand that they were in no danger of starving, and that they were guaranteed to receive as much treatment as we could provide. It takes time for a human to get back on their feet after they have suffered almost unbearable blows. Rather than trying to soothe them with solicitous attention, the better thing to do in this case was to let them wail so they could release the built-up pain in their sorrow-stricken hearts.

Thus, little by little the women took a turn for the better. It would be

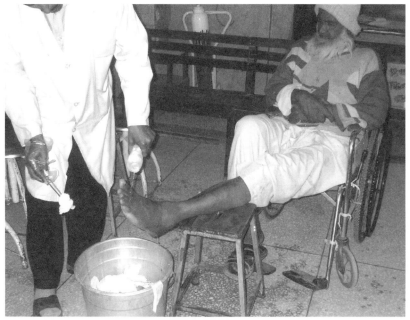

Hansen's disease patient receiving treatment.

The author (at far left) with patients being treated at the ward.

easy for me to leave it at that, but the fact of the matter was that, with us all crowded together in that small ward, listening to the pained cries of those women demanded enormous stoicism and patience from my staff, the other patients, and me.

After about six months, the mother and the older sister had managed to achieve a respite from their condition and left, able to smile again. If the story ended here, it would be a moving account of healing. But there is more to this tale.

Harima, left behind in the ward, was tormented by repeated lepra reactions. Her voice was rough due to an edema of the larynx, and she frequently suffered from breathing difficulties and bouts of pneumonia. At this time, we were unable to get our hands on the specific medicine for lepra reactions. There was nothing for us to do but ignore her as she pitifully cried, "Please kill me!" and wait for her symptoms to subside. The dark question I quietly asked myself was whether I should let her develop severe pneumonia and wait for her to die, or somehow force her to keep going. It was not easy to try to distract this patient with little jokes and offer consoling words.

Several months later, I could no longer ignore her strained breathing, and so I performed a tracheotomy, opening a hole in her throat so she could breathe directly through her windpipe. Naturally, although her respiratory difficulties were alleviated, she lost her voice. This would make it difficult for her to fully reenter society.

The question of whether this patient—this human being named Harima— would be happy with such an outcome left me somber for quite a while. Furthermore, the situation in Afghanistan and Peshawar was quite desperate at the time, making me question nearly all of my optimistic convictions and judgments regarding human beings. I did not know what to do with the unfamiliar emotions surging up from the dark depths inside me—emotions I could not even identify, whether as anger or sorrow. The human condition— it was impossible for me to find an answer with my meager brain. That said, I am sure that Harima herself had the same questions. Coming from a person whose only words were prayers to God, those forthright cries themselves were most eloquent.

I, too, was just another lowly, confused human being, living awash in the mud of life along with our patients. The only thing that I was certain of was the fact that, even if I had acquired some clever theories and skills and was respected as "Doctor Sahib" ("Sahib" is the honorific used for men), I was still on the same level as the crying, screaming Harima.

The dark Christmas of 1985 is one that I will never forget. The Soviet army was pushing toward the Khyber Pass on the outskirts of Peshawar.

A fierce battle broke out at the top of the pass, and vehicles carrying the wounded were going back and forth between hospitals around the city and the pass throughout the day and night. The residents were terrified by the incessant sound of explosives. The winter rainy season had begun, and the skies over Peshawar were filled with heavy gray clouds. The constant roar of distant cannons could be heard in the city. People who could not return to their hometowns—or who had lost them entirely—filled the ward and its verandas. Since we could not accommodate everyone, we put up tents and put beds in them, and had some people sleep there.

Around that time, a certain Japanese organization conducting overseas medical cooperation sent me a succession of pressing demands to attend an "important conference" in a distant country. There were no mobile phones or Internet connections then; correspondence depended entirely on the mail. It took about one week for a letter to get from Tokyo to Peshawar, and even then, only about 70 percent of the correspondence got through, so I probably did not even receive all of their missives. The letters said things like, "We would like you to share your experiences as an overseas worker with us, based on the realities of being in a developing country, and as someone living with people at the grassroots in Asia. . . . Let us have a conversation in an Asian mountain village surrounded by its people and the beauties of nature. . . ."

I was struck by the hollowness of these words. What was real to me was not this kind of beautifully embellished language, but the despair of Harima as she screamed and begged God for relief. Furthermore, in this time of emergency, there was no way a clinician could leave his patients behind for an extended time; given the security situation, it would also be dangerous to bring along my family as requested and move about. As much as I tried to explain the circumstances, the organizers seemed incapable of understanding. There was much useless back-and-forth chatter and argument. When I received what looked like the final notice requesting my attendance, I impulsively tore it up. At that moment, I made a clean break with the world of "overseas medical cooperation" activities consisting mainly of events and debates lacking in substance.

Seeking the Water of Life
1986–2001

Chapter 3

Opening Clinics amid a Civil War

Refugees from a Brutal War

When I took up my position in Peshawar, Pakistan, in 1984, a frightful inter-necine conflict was raging just across the border in neighboring Afghanistan.

In 1973, former prime minister and royal family member Mohammed Daoud Khan had overthrown the monarchy and established a republican government. His aim was to modernize Afghanistan, a "museum piece" among the countries of the world. But Daoud and his family were killed in a coup d'état launched by young left-wing military officers. This group quickly established a radical communist regime and harshly suppressed anti-government Islamists. People throughout the country revolted against these measures, and factional conflicts within the government itself also grew fierce. The Soviet Union, judging that the regime was in danger of collapse, intervened militarily on a large scale in December 1979; more than 100,000 Soviet troops had been dispatched by the start of 1982.

The Soviets, along with the forces of the communist government, implemented a policy of wanton violence. This involved thoroughly destroying village communities, which were seen as hotbeds of "feudalism," and forcing people into the cities where they could be controlled. It is said that around 5,000 settlements were destroyed by the bombing and the shelling, and around half of the country's farm villages were pummeled. Some 750,000 people had died as a direct result of the war by the time the Soviet army withdrew in 1989. If indirect casualties are included, the number rises to two million. Villagers began fleeing the country en masse to escape the attacks, constituting the first large-scale wave of refugees. It is reported that by 1985, some 2.7 million people had taken refuge in Pakistan (primarily in the North-West Frontier Province) and upwards of 1.5 million had fled to Iran.

The supposedly overwhelming military strength of the Soviet forces turned out to be vastly overrated. Contrary to general expectations, the Afghan country farmers armed with old rifles who formed the main body of the resistance were able in many places to rout government and Soviet forces equipped with modern armaments. The United States got seriously involved once it

Soviet tanks in Afghanistan.

Refugees escaping the battlefront.

became clear that the farmer-soldiers were putting up a good fight. A law passed by the US Congress in August 1984 provided for the supply of arms to support the Afghan "freedom fighters." A US military training facility was established on the outskirts of Peshawar, and Stinger missiles appeared on the scene in 1986. This intervention changed the character of the conflict. The rural resistance forces became affiliated with political factions, and their corps of rifle-toting farmers were replaced by contingents of professional jihadis— mercenaries in the pay of the factions. (Incidentally, the word "jihad," often translated as "holy war," originally referred to a struggle to protect the faith, and this did not necessarily involve the use of arms.)

Afghan resistance factions set up their headquarters across the border in Peshawar, and with assistance from the Central Intelligence Agency and the Pakistani military, they recruited an international volunteer force to support their cause. A contingent of volunteers rushed to the scene from Arab countries; these men, who came to be known as "Afghan Arabs," were the predecessor to Al Qaeda. Being home to the headquarters of several resistance groups, along with the consulates of the United States, Iran, Afghanistan, and the Soviet Union, Peshawar was in a state of pandemonium.

Out in the countryside, villages split into factions and villagers began fighting among themselves. As a result, the traditional order of the Afghan farm village fell apart. In Kunar Province to the east, as the government army gradually withdrew from the border areas, the Arab-led fighters, the forces of local farmers and their former feudal lords, and the factions reliant on US aid vied with one another for dominance. The destruction of rural communities continued, and many farming families who had remained now also fled into adjacent Pakistani territory. Similar developments were apparently taking place all around Afghanistan. With foreign intervention making the situation impossibly complicated, people became exhausted by the deadly struggle and began to harbor doubts.

Laying the Groundwork for Opening Our Clinics

We, too, were sucked into this vortex as providers of medical care. As I mentioned earlier, the Pashtuns are the largest of Afghanistan's ethnic groups. They also form an overwhelming majority in Pakistan's North-West Frontier Province (Khyber Pakhtunkhwa). Pashtuns are said to constitute the world's largest tribal society, with some 16 million people spread across the two countries; the national border holds little meaning for them. More than half of the patients in our ward were of Afghan nationality, and were therefore not beneficiaries of the Pakistani government's Hansen's disease eradication plan.

In 1986, we founded the Afghan Leprosy Service (ALS) in Peshawar and began treatment activities on a modest scale in the area's refugee camps. As we did so, we made a major policy change. In districts without doctors, the places where Hansen's disease was common were also areas where other infectious diseases, such as typhoid, malaria, tuberculosis, and amoebic dysentery, were prevalent. We could not refuse to treat a half-dead malaria patient just because they were not suffering from Hansen's disease. Furthermore, upon querying patients where they had come from, we found out that most were from isolated mountain villages where medical facilities were nonexistent.

Based on these circumstances, we decided that once the civil war had waned sufficiently, we would build clinics in Afghan mountain villages where both Hansen's disease and other infectious diseases frequently occurred, and we would provide general medical care there. Hansen's disease would simply be one of the conditions we treated. Our grand objective was to establish a model system of medical care for Afghan mountain villages that had no medical care infrastructure. And we began vigorous efforts toward that goal.

The first step was to develop friendly relations with residents of the areas where we planned to set up clinics. In 1988, I selected twenty of the younger Afghan refugees and began training them to be medical staffers. We began looking around the Dara-e-Noor Valley in Nangarhar Province, which was where I planned to build our first clinic two years later. I also investigated the northeastern mountainous regions of backcountry Dara-e-Pech and Wama.

The Road to Dara-e-Noor

Early in the morning of November 26, 1991, I left Peshawar together with four members of the Japan-Afghanistan Medical Service (JAMS) (JAMS was the successor to the Afghan Leprosy Service [ALS], and later merged with Peace Japan Medical Services [PMS]). Our job was to carry out the final survey of the planned site and make a final decision on the plan. We went from the Mohmand Agency in Pakistan to the foothills of the 2,500-meter-high Mithai Pass, and we then tried to enter Kunar in Afghanistan on foot. Unfortunately, road traffic had been cut off by fighting between guerrilla groups, making it impractical to travel by motor vehicle. This blockage also led to major delays in implementation of our plans for clinics further inside Afghanistan. Meanwhile, however, our Afghan team members had been earnestly vying with each other to polish their skills over the previous three years, and to keep their spirits from lagging I needed to reach a firm decision without further delay.

Peace Japan Medical Services (PMS) Clinics in Afghanistan

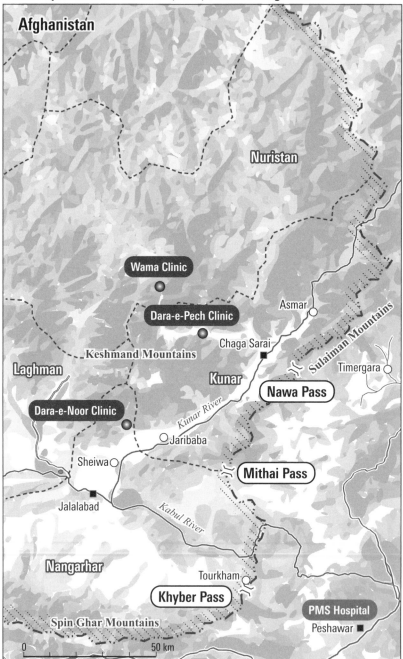

We began careful planning for the clinics in Afghanistan around the end of 1988. On January 1, 1989, we launched a program for training clinic staff; our trainees came from the areas where we planned to open clinics. We then waited for the strife to cool down. In November 1990, we opened a branch office in Timergara, along the border to the north of Peshawar. We organized a rotating shift system of deployments so staff members could build up some experience, and this laid the foundations for us to open clinics within Afghanistan.

By 1991, the civil war had waned. With signs pointing toward relative political stability, we began making serious preparations for opening clinics. I decided that we would open our first clinic in Afghanistan in the lower reaches of a branch of the Kunar River in the Dara-e-Noor valley, and that we would do so on December 1. That August and September, two groups went to scout locations and provide field care. In the process, one member of our staff was killed in Sheiwa, downstream from our target site. The opening of the planned clinic came to represent a critical test of our determination.

Our target site was in a gorge along the Kunar River. Viewed from Peshawar, it was just on the other side of the Sulaiman Mountains to the west. One reason why we targeted this area was that more than half of the Afghan Hansen's disease sufferers being registered in Peshawar were from areas along the Kunar River. And 70 to 80 percent of the cases from there were clustered in the northwestern river basin region of Dara-e-Pech. It was the single largest focus of the Hansen's disease eradication plan.

Accordingly, we decided to base ourselves in the neighboring Dara-e-Noor Valley, located on the other side of the Keshmand Mountains to the south of Dara-e-Pech. Our plan was to spend a year or so to set up a model medical treatment system in that valley while waiting for the general situation to calm down. Given that we could naturally expect small groups of people from Dara-e-Pech to come across the mountains through the pass to get here, we would be able to gather information from them about the situation there. If the competing factions settled down, we anticipated being able to start fullfledged operations in Dara-e-Pech; if the situation remained unstable, we would still be able to provide assistance from our base on the Dara-e-Noor side of the mountains.

Contrary to our expectations, however, the political chaos worsened, and we lost contact with Dara-e-Noor. Our third reconnoitering party returned in October. After that, the factional fighting became even fiercer. The Nawa Pass—the main traffic route used in place of the Khyber Pass—had been closed, and nearly a month had passed. Usually, JAMS put a premium on caution and did everything it could to avoid taking unnecessary risks.

However, we also had to avoid making local residents think we had betrayed them. Opinions were divided: some favored postponement of our plans; others thought we should go ahead. I was in the latter camp. "The die is cast," I declared, saying we should start on schedule, operating first on a small scale, gathering information, and then expanding our activities as we could without undue haste. I thought that we should put down roots at the proposed site with a view to being there for decades.

However, the site surveys we did to prepare for setting up our clinic did not give us an accurate grasp either of the valley's population or of the damage that had been caused by the civil war. Much of what was reported was no more than vague impressions. If we were going to draft a real plan, we would need to conduct a more precise survey in order both to decide on the scale of our activities and to win the approval of our financial backers in Japan. And so it transpired that I myself was to survey the site and make the final decision.

Meanwhile, the Soviets had begun their withdrawal in May 1988 and had pulled out all 90,000 of their troops by the following February. The world was abuzz with the news of this pullout, and a stream of United Nations organs and nongovernmental organizations (NGOs)—reportedly over two hundred in total—set up shop in Peshawar. People were under the false impression that the Soviet withdrawal would lead immediately to the return of the refugees and Afghanistan's reconstruction. But in fact, the civil conflict grew ever more intractable. With the start of the Gulf War in January 1991, the international groups dispersed like baby spiders scattered by the wind, and the projects that various countries had launched were stopped. This was a decisive factor in cementing distrust of foreigners among Afghan refugees.

Regardless of these developments, however, we kept up our activities without a break, and after all of the hard work described above, in December 1991 we began making preparations to open our clinic in the Dara-e-Noor Valley village of Qal'ah-ye Shahi in northern Jalalabad. Staff members from the area played a leading role, and with the help of their regional and blood ties they managed to visit every nook and cranny of the valley. Meanwhile, we put the bulk of our Afghan team to work on converting a house into a medical facility, and in March 1992 our first clinic within Afghanistan was established.

The following month, the communist government of President Mohammad Najibullah in Kabul collapsed. In the aftermath, the political forces based in the provinces that had been receiving support from the US military began to converge on the capital with the goal of achieving power. The battlefields moved from farm villages to the city. The refugees—the majority of whom were farmers—realized that it had become possible to restore the traditional

The author on horseback in a caravan headed out for a mobile treatment mission in a mountainous region near the Wakhan Corridor in northern Pakistan.

At the top of the Mithai Pass, crossing the border into Afghanistan. The author is in the center.

autonomy of their farm villages, and began streaming home in astonishing numbers. According to the United Nations High Commissioner for Refugees (UNHCR), over the six-month period from July through December 1992, some 2 million of the estimated 2.7 million Afghan refugees in Pakistan made their way home. Almost all of them did so of their own volition and through their own efforts.

Beyond Ethnic Groups

The Dara-e-Noor Valley is in a mountainous region of northern Nangarhar Province. It forms a triangular area separated from neighboring Laghman and Kunar provinces by the Keshmand Mountains, which rise to a height of approximately 4,000 meters. One of the reasons we chose this valley for our first clinic was that there was a shortage of medical care facilities in the area. In addition, as I have already mentioned, we knew there were many Hansen's disease sufferers living along the Kunar River. And most importantly, our lead Afghan physician had told us that this was a strategic point from which we could serve all three of the above-mentioned provinces. It may have appeared that way on the map, but on traveling through the area with staff, I learned that getting across the valley requires a two-day trip through a pass at an elevation of more than 4,000 meters. It is not a route for regular human traffic. The valley, which is inhabited by Pashai, a hill people numbering around 30,000, is nearly completely enclosed.

In short, Dara-e-Noor was a location selected due to a lack of sufficient research on our part. I realized that even Afghans do not know every nook and cranny of their own country. If you think about it, it is the same thing as a person from Tokyo not knowing anything about the mountains in Kyushu or the dialect spoken there. Many of our Afghan physicians were from Kabul, the capital, and they were fearful of the Pashtun and Pashai living deep in the mountains. They were reluctant to work in Dara-e-Noor and refused to be posted to the new clinic. This made our staff members from the area angry, and our medical team faced rough going from the start.

The physicians from Kabul wanted us to open a clinic on the outskirts of the city of Jalalabad, but I refused without hesitation. I ordered that we proceed in accordance with our announced plan, under which we were to set up "clinics for mountain villages in districts without doctors." It would not do for our plan to be a sham. The physicians who refused assignment to Dara-e-Noor dangled the threat of resignation as a show of opposition. I countered by firing them—more than a dozen people in all. This came as an unexpected shock to

The first clinic, opened in Dara-e-Noor.

The second clinic, opened in Dara-e-Pech.

them. Around this time many foreign NGOs had been pulling out of Pesha-war after having been around for just a few years. The Afghans working for these organizations—in particular, those from the intellectual classes who had fled from Kabul—were aware of this transience, and their idea was just to keep the foreigners happy for a while and get something out of it for themselves.

My move quelled the disturbance, but these kinds of firmly held prej-udices are not simply dispelled with some persuasion. I took the lead and went ahead with providing treatment. It was a matter of "don't argue—just do it." In the process of continuing to provide actual medical care, our staff gradually began to let go of their preconceptions about the area, and their prejudices went away. And so, our now self-confident Afghan medical team headed out further into the backcountry to Dara-e-Pech.

On November 4, 1992, I set out from Dara-e-Noor with my principal team members to start concrete negotiations with the residents of the area where we planned to open our second clinic. The site, Dara-e-Pech, is an eight-hour trek from Chaga Sarai (Asadabad), the capital of Kunar Province. Two tributaries join to form the Kunar River at Chaga Sarai, and Dara-e-Pech is the long, deep valley that runs through the mountainous region northwest of there. The valley is vast—tens of times larger than Dara-e-Noor—and its backcountry forms the heartland of Nuristan. Countless massifs of all sizes range alongside it. The name "Dara-e-Pech" means "crooked valley," and in keeping with this, the river running through it follows a serpentine course while being fed by numerous tributaries. As elsewhere, Pashtun occupy the basin areas along the main river, while members of various local tribes reside in the higher-altitude mountain regions.

As we traveled upstream, the waters became clearer and the people less sophisticated. Rice harvesting in the cultivated lands along the river had just ended, and here and there the leaves on trees were turning colors in the late-autumn chill. There were communities with anywhere from several dozen to up to maybe one hundred households every kilometer or so, and in the places where roads had been repaired and travel was possible, almost all the farmers had returned. However, in the war-ravaged locations where transpor-tation conditions were poor, communities lay in ruins everywhere, present-ing pitiful scenes of devastation. Why had such thoroughgoing destruction been wrought in these peaceful mountain recesses? I could not help but think about the hardships that residents must have faced earlier when they fled to Pakistan on foot along these arduous mountain routes.

In December 1992, deliveries of equipment gradually began getting through, and we started selecting staff members from the local population. Two years later, we set up our third clinic in Afghanistan, located in the

The Wama Clinic, the most remote of the three PMS facilities in Afghanistan.

At the top of the Mithai Pass, crossing the border into Afghanistan. The author is in the center.

village of Wama, Nuristan. For nearly a dozen years—until January 2005, when travel became impossible owing to the US army's "terrorist suppression" activities—we kept our clinics in Dara-e-Pech and Wama in operation, winning immeasurable trust from local residents. The Afghan staffers who had sympathized with our plans and cooperated in setting up the clinics remained strong allies afterward as well. The totally sincere bonds that we formed with such people made it possible for us to work together—even under circumstances where lives could be at stake—and surmount the obstacles we faced.

Chapter 4

Persevering through Drought and Air Strikes

The Great Afghan Drought

After we completed a round of improvements to the Hansen's disease ward of the Mission Hospital in Peshawar, a dispute arose among those implementing the Hansen's disease eradication plan, and in response to political considerations a declaration was issued that the eradication effort had been completed. As a result, the flow of funds that we had relied on from foreign organizations was cut, and the Mission Hospital itself was on the verge of collapse. Accordingly, we at the Peshawar-kai decided that we could no longer rely on the space lent to us by the Mission Hospital. In 1998—fifteen years after the start of our activities on the ground there—we built a new seventy-bed facility in Peshawar at our own expense, naming it the PMS (Peshawar-kai Medical Services; later changed to Peace Japan Medical Services) Hospital. In addition, we decided to localize our operations in the form of a social welfare corporation. These steps made it possible for us to maintain operations in both Afghanistan and Pakistan so long as the Peshawar-kai in Japan continued to exist.

In Afghanistan, political chaos had continued after the Soviets pulled out in 1989, but in 1996 the Taliban, an Islamist force, took control in Kabul. With this, the odds that the entire country would be brought under unified rule increased at a single stroke, and it seemed that the end of the civil war was at hand.

The spring of 2000 saw the whole of Central Asia experience an unprecedented drought. That May, the World Health Organization (WHO) called attention to the horrific situation. The UN organization sounded the alarm that Afghanistan had become the site of the most severe suffering. More than half of the population—around twelve million people—had been affected in some way by the drought. Four million people were on the verge of starvation, and a million were at the edge of death. Food production had dropped by more than half, and farmlands were turning into deserts. Ninety percent of the country's livestock had died, and farming families were abandoning their villages and becoming displaced persons. This was the second mass exodus of refugees in the country, following on the one resulting from the Soviet-Afghan War that started in 1979. At least one million people are said to have fled. In addition, our clinics were caught in the conflict between Taliban and anti-Taliban forces, as the ebb and flow of their struggle for supremacy continued. The situation seemed apocalyptic.

Seeking Water

Under these conditions, our clinics saw a noticeable increase in the number of young mothers coming in bearing toddlers near death. Many of the drought's victims were little children. Death from starvation is not due to an empty stomach, but to the malnutrition caused by insufficient food, which lowers the body's resistance to disease. If polluted drinking water is added to the equation, a person can become afflicted with an enteric infection such as diarrhea and easily lose their life. Sometimes these young women had been walking for days to get to the clinic with a child near death. It was not unusual to see mothers who had managed to reach a clinic with their child still alive, only to have that child die in their embrace as they waited in line to be checked in. No person with children of their own could help weeping at the sight of these bereft mothers standing there looking dazed.

And so, in July 2000, I took to heart the urgings of the Afghan physicians at the Dara-e-Noor clinic, who had become absolutely desperate. Recognizing that this was no longer the moment to be focused on curing illnesses, the clinic shifted its priority to obtaining clean drinking water. The fact is, most of the illnesses we dealt with could have been avoided if people had an adequate supply of food and clean drinking water. We assembled the villagers who remained and got to work digging deep wells. That August, we established the PMS Water Supply Office in Jalalabad to specifically handle the problem, and we launched a well-digging effort in the drought-plagued areas of Nangarhar Province. The people who took the lead in realizing our goals were young Japanese workers who were volunteering at the time at the PMS Hospital in Peshawar, like Hasuoka Osamu and Meguro Susumu.

It was the stability of the PMS Hospital that made these activities possible. Thanks to the extraordinary efforts of our long-term Japanese workers, including those responsible for accounting and for nursing, we had finally overcome the disorganization that had characterized the facility in its startup phase. It goes without saying that we also had support from the staff at our administrative office in Japan, who were constantly trying to raise awareness of the desperate situation in Afghanistan, as well as financial support

Children drinking the scant muddy water remaining in a river. The lack of water took the lives of many children.

from Peshawar-kai members who unhesitatingly donated enormous sums of money. All of these elements came together and made it possible to undertake this new project.

People had fallen into a state of almost total desperation, and they all lent a hand regardless of whether they were pro- or anti-Taliban. Though I talk of "well-digging," in fact the wells themselves had already long existed, but they had run dry, and would not produce water despite the farmers' efforts. The reason for this quickly became apparent when we started digging and ran into a stratum of boulders less than 20 meters down. Pickaxes were no use for penetrating a geological layer of calf-sized boulders. After a lot of trial and error, we found that the most effective approach was to open holes in the large boulders with a jackhammer, pack them with explosives, and shatter the boulders into pieces. When we found unexploded rocket shells and land mines, we would scrape out the explosive material and put it to peaceful use. As luck would have it, our team included farmers-turned-soldiers who had become skilled at explosives as guerrillas during the civil war, and their abilities were a great help.

We had dozens of young local employees working in groups led by young

Locations of Well-Digging Activities around Nangarhar Province

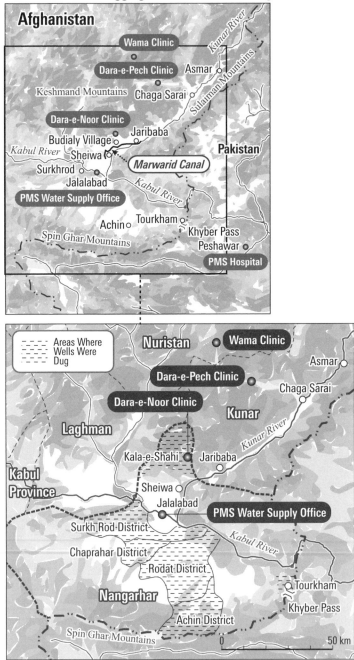

Japanese volunteers, and they quickly expanded the number of locations where we did our work. As of October 2000, we had dug wells at 274 locations. By September 2001 we were up to 660 wells, more than 90 percent of which produced water. This activity continued without cessation even during the US "retaliatory strikes" in Afghanistan, which I will talk about later. Even after the Japanese volunteers left, the people who remained carried on with the work. By 2004, wells had been dug in more than 1,000 locations; by 2006 the figure had risen to around 1,600. The well-digging had turned into a major project that helped people from dozens of villages remain in place rather than migrating elsewhere.

Water for Irrigation

Providing villagers with water to drink was not enough. As Afghan farm villages are almost entirely self-sufficient, residents could not survive if they were unable to grow crops. The numbers of farmers leaving their villages to seek cash income had not changed one bit. More than a few of those who departed had become mercenaries serving on the front lines of the civil war. Accordingly, at PMS we promoted the idea of returning Afghan farm villages to their original state in order to lay the foundations for health and peace, and we worked at restoring farmland that had experienced desertification. Our greatest objective was to get water for irrigation, and that effort centered on the Dara-e-Noor Valley.

A *karez* is a type of horizontal well that draws groundwater out through a tunnel that stretches for 100 meters or more. For irrigation, this method is tremendously effective. We got to work on repairing *karez* in the Dara-e-Noor Valley, and succeeded in returning thirty-eight out of forty to working order. The desertified farmland in the vicinity of our clinic was revived in short order, and around a hundred families came back to the land. I recognized at this time just how great the blessings of water are. Even though I was the one who had issued the instructions to work on the wells, I was surprised by the wonderful results.

Furthermore, recognizing that even the *karez* had limits, we also set about digging wells that were more than 5 meters in diameter for irrigation purposes, and brought several dozen more hectares into cultivation. In this way, we gradually revived the fields in the valley around the clinic, and the number of people who resumed farming increased.

But then the water table began to fall. This brought home the fact that this drought was not an ordinary one, and our sense of crisis became more acute.

The author lowering himself to the bottom of an irrigation well he helped dig.

Water drawn up from an irrigation well being discharged onto farmland.

The September 11 Attacks

Despite this calamity, international relief efforts to deal with the drought were nowhere to be seen. Meanwhile, Al Qaeda—which was being sheltered by the Taliban government—had become a troublesome presence. The United States and the United Kingdom directed their hostility at Afghanistan, and in January 2001 the United Nations strengthened its sanctions on the country. Because of the lack of international awareness of the drought and famine, foodstuffs were initially included among the sanctioned items, though UN staff members in Afghanistan who were familiar with the reality of the situation fiercely opposed this measure.

As then–Foreign Minister Wakil Ahmed Muttawakil later explained, this was a turning point. Most within the Taliban government had stressed being prudent, but at this point there was an about-face and extremist views came to dominate. The destruction of the Buddhist statuary at Bamyan happened shortly thereafter, in March 2001. Meanwhile, throngs of starving people crossed the borders in greater numbers, and the refugee population grew.

In Kabul, the various Western groups that might have provided aid to the drought refugees pulled out one after another. The water levels at the wells were falling rapidly in the capital just as they had in the eastern region, as was evident in the places that were running out of water. In densely populated areas like Dashte Barchi, where many Hazaras live, enteric infections caused by unhygienic conditions, such as dysentery and infectious skin diseases like leishmaniasis, had become oppressively rife. By March 2001, Kabul was in serious need of medical facilities, and so PMS hastily established temporary clinics in five locations.

However, five temporary clinics represented just a drop in the bucket. I directed staff to make preparations to increase the number of clinic locations to ten within the year, as well as to rapidly add another 1,000 water-supply locations to the 660 that had already been completed in Nangarhar Province. On September 10, I made a brief return to Peshawar. The following day, I received an urgent phone call from Jalalabad, informing me of the terrorist attacks in New York and Washington, DC.

Neither Hasuoka Osamu nor Meguro Susumu, the Japanese staffers who were overseeing the well project, had any thoughts of immediately leaving the country. Jalalabad was already accustomed to the chaos of war and air strikes. I was sure that there would be no upheavals big enough to be reported in the foreign media, and the situation seemed calm.

We Will Come Back

On September 13, I returned to Jalalabad in haste. There, I gathered together our eighty-seven staff members and explained what our plan of action would be. I told Hasuoka and Meguro to pack up and leave Jalalabad within three days, go to Peshawar, and wait there.

Anticipating a large-scale military reprisal, I had our vehicles and equipment moved to a location we thought would be safe. I had the medical supplies moved to the Dara-e-Noor Valley, where we had a PMS clinic, ordering everyone to be prepared to stay hunkered down for several months. I sent an order to the five Kabul clinics directing staff whose families were in Peshawar to return there, while those whose families were in Kabul were to decide for themselves whether to stay in the capital or leave.

Our office overseeing the work of securing water supplies—the heart of our drought-relief effort—was in Jalalabad; our young workers from Japan were also staying there. Despite the fourteenth being a Friday and thus a day off from work, all of the staff at the PMS Water Supply Office were brought together at seven o'clock that morning for an unusual assembly.

The city was surprisingly tranquil that day, and people were placidly going about their routine activities. Even so, they were well aware of the situation. As usual, the BBC Pashto service was broadcasting news about the moves of the US, and all of the staff had a far more accurate assessment of what was happening than the Japanese public did. Three years prior, Jalalabad had been a major target of US cruise missile attacks, and residents knew full well that the air strikes would be on an even bigger scale this time.

People seemed to be quietly preparing for whatever was to come. Rather than heated rhetoric expressing hatred of America and promoting the will to fight, what I heard was talk of just surviving another day and entrusting the rest to God. Though there was tension behind their determination, there was no sense whatsoever that anyone was panicking or expressing intense antagonism.

I briefly explained the situation to the assembled Japanese employees. Hasuoka asked me to give our local staffers a plausible excuse for the evacuation of the Japanese workers and encourage them to keep up their morale. When I spoke to them, I became sentimental. "I want to thank you," I said, "for your efforts over this past year. Through that work, you helped more than 200,000 people stay in their villages and avoid death. As you have already heard, this city is exposed to danger from retaliatory strikes launched by the US. However, we will come back. PMS is not going to abandon you. We must not fear death. However, our deaths must have meaning for other people.

Once the crisis is over, let us sweat and work together once again. Take this week off and use it to prepare for the evacuation of your families. Work will resume on September 23. There will be absolutely no changes to our project."

Ghulam Sakhi, a staff member who went by the nickname "Tarafdar" and had a face that showed the wisdom of his years, stood up to express his gratitude. "My friends, there are just two types of people in the world: those who think of others unselfishly and those whose hearts are clouded by designs for how they will profit. I think we know which type PMS belongs to. We will never forget you Japanese and your country."

These would be our parting words.

None of the staff members who had family in Afghanistan attempted to flee to Peshawar. I could not help but feel ashamed deep down in my heart at their composure and their smiling faces. I hugged the one physician who was taking his own life in his hands by setting out for Kabul. "May God protect you," I said as I saw him off. We both knew that there was no chance of our meeting again.

After I arrived back in Japan, the structure of the US-Taliban confrontation that had the whole country in a frenzy somehow struck me as contrived. I could not forget the image of people back in Afghanistan calmly going about their daily lives.

My "More Harm Than Good" Declaration

Further developments had a detrimental effect on the situation in and around Afghanistan. The retaliatory bombings that the US and the UK insisted on conducting became quite intense. The Japanese government secured enactment of its Anti-Terrorism Special Measures Law and decided it would dispatch the Self-Defense Forces (SDF) to the region. And in response to a US-UK request for assistance, Tokyo also dispatched an SDF Aegis-equipped destroyer to the Indian Ocean.

On October 13, 2001, prior to the passage of the Special Measures Law, I was asked to speak to a special committee of the House of Representatives in the National Diet—an institution at the very core of Japan's political system, a world that was completely alien to me. We ordinarily avoided interacting with the world of politics. But I thought this would provide me with a rare opportunity to inform politicians about the realities of the drought and ask for some sort of food distribution program, so I willingly consented. My intention was to convey the facts at hand and turn the well-meaning prayers for peace into positive energy. I did not want to engage in a sterile battle over concepts. Making peace requires greater active effort than making war.

In Afghanistan, the harsh winter was bearing down on communities already in the hell of starvation. The urgent issue for this country was not one of politics or military matters. It was a problem of bread and water. Life is precious—this is a universal fact. That was all I wanted to say.

The debate going on in the Diet at the time concerned the government's proposal to dispatch the SDF "in order to protect NGOs engaged in aid activities at refugee camps." In my comments to the special committee, I did not present any abstract arguments. Instead, I spoke about current conditions in Afghanistan, in particular about the misery caused by the great drought and the plight of the Afghan refugees. I made the appeal that famine relief was needed more than any SDF dispatch.

The majority of the people I had seen in Kabul could well have been described as displaced persons from farm villages. The city's middle-class population had long since fled from danger by crossing over to Peshawar and other places in Pakistan. In short, one could say the people remaining in Kabul were those who could not escape to take refuge in another country.

I told the committee, "If troops were sent from Japan on the basis of shaky information, local residents would see a uniformed contingent and sense something strange. Accordingly, dispatching the SDF would do more harm than good. Dealing with the famine situation is the most urgent issue at hand."

This statement unleashed a commotion in the chamber. The representatives seated directly across from me were suddenly in an uproar. They began heckling me and showering me with ridicule and jeers. The Diet member serving as chair demanded that I retract my statement. It was as though dispatching the SDF was the obvious policy to adopt and my summons as an unsworn witness was a mere formality.

Still, I went on: "Anti-Japanese sentiment will worsen at one stroke. [Dispatching the SDF] will destroy the lessons [of pacifism] that our predecessors spilled their blood to learn. In conclusion, I appeal to everyone here who is a father or a mother, regardless of which party you belong to. To repeat: the urgent issue is how to deal with the great drought and famine." With that, I concluded my bid for a project to provide food aid.

Distributing Food under Bombardment

There were actually many people in Japan who shunned the idea of Japanese cooperation with the war effort and heeded explanations of what was really going on in Afghanistan. The Peshawar-kai's appeal for emergency food assis-

Villagers leaving their drought-stricken town behind.

Well-digging work continued even under bombardment.

tance generated an unprecedented response. Our financial staff were initially taken aback by my public appeal for contributions when I stated, "We could reduce the number of people facing immediate starvation if we had one or two hundred million yen." Their pessimism about the prospects for raising that much turned out to be unfounded. Donations had already exceeded my 200-million-yen target by the end of the month (October 2001), and by January 2002 the figure had reached close to 600 million yen (equivalent to nearly US$5 million).

In this way we were able to solidify our financial base. When I returned to Peshawar on October 18, I left behind instructions to send the funds along speedily without concern for the budget. The supplies of wheat flour and cooking oil for the crucial emergency food assistance project had already been purchased in Peshawar and were ready to be shipped out. I had wanted to send them out in volume before the air strikes began, but that turned out not to be possible. Jalalabad was bombed on October 7, and it was only a matter of time before serious strikes on Kabul would begin. Under these conditions, I had some apprehension over who would participate in the distribution effort, but twenty staffers volunteered to participate in a team led by the hospital's assistant director, Dr. Ziaur-Rahman, and Tarafdar (Ghulam Sakhi), who had been a military academy instructor.

Distributing food to the starving people who descended on the relief team presented numerous difficulties. The staff could not tell who was truly in need. Also, the so-called pinpoint strikes speciously reported in Japan—which supposedly hit only places where terrorists were, leaving civilian residents unharmed—were in fact indiscriminate bombing raids. It was true, though, that certain districts were selected for systematic bombing. One such district would be attacked intensely, and so people would flee, only to see the next place they had thought was safe get attacked. The residents ran this way and that day and night, trying to escape on foot, by taxi, and by horse-drawn cart, and their nerves were worn down. Naturally, there were many casualties. The conflict was like a completely one-sided game of murder. The destitute Taliban regime lacked any weaponry of consequence other than rifles, swords, and anti-tank guns. Its only airpower consisted of a few helicopters. Japanese newspapers ran stories with earnest headlines such as "US Secures Air Superiority" and "Allied Occupation of Japan Being Considered as Model for Postwar Afghanistan." Militarily, however, with a foe that posed virtually no resistance, one could say that the war was just an act.

Even International Red Cross facilities that could be clearly distinguished from the air took direct hits and were severely damaged, while the offices used by Al Jazeera—the only media outlet to continue broadcasting reports on the

Rations of wheat and cooking oil being distributed to starving refugees in Kabul. The PMS relief effort continued while the city was under bombardment.

air strikes—were demolished. We were concerned that it would no longer be possible to distribute food if even one bomb struck the quarters where our volunteer team members lived.

Accordingly, I gave strict orders that our distribution team split their living quarters up into three locations around the city. That way, if one group was dealt a crushing blow, the other two would be able to carry on with their duties. With that, we began our distribution work from three different directions, all focused mainly on Dashte Barchi in Kabul's outskirts, where Hazara people lived. Bombs dropped nearly on top of the PMS team's quarters in the Mikroyan district, and many local residents were killed, but the volunteers unflinchingly continued their work. Our five clinics around the city likewise continued their mission without a break, serving as an encouraging presence for residents.

The Fall of Kabul and the Entry of the "Liberation Army"

On the evening of November 12, the Taliban authorities issued a notice calling for a prompt pullout from Kabul. The following day, all Taliban units and people involved with their government suddenly disappeared. It was clearly a move planned in advance. The foreigners from Christian groups and media organizations who had been detained prior to the bombing were released as though by agreement at the Tourkham border crossing immediately thereafter.

When I returned to Japan, I found that the Afghan situation as it was being reported in the media was completely different from what we were seeing in Afghanistan itself. The images that created the greatest misunderstanding were those depicting people "released from Taliban oppression" cheering and welcoming the entry of the Northern Alliance army, followed by pictures of women removing their burka. These video clips were broadcast over and over ad nauseam. But they were an illusion. Some five years before, in September 1996, those same people had cheered and welcomed the victorious Taliban forces as they entered Kabul. The situation was the same in Jalalabad, where I was at the time. For most of the people shown "welcoming" the Northern Alliance forces, this response was nothing more than a declaration of their intention not to fight. Depending on the district, the flags of the Hamid Karzai government, the Northern Alliance, and the Taliban might all be flying amicably side by side. People in Kabul had lost many family members and other kin in the bombing. For them, the arrival of these latest conquerors can hardly have been a pleasant event. They actually had a terribly jaded view of the scene.

And so did I. I could not help but be astonished at this world based on fabrications and delusions. And I grew tired of talking about the truth. No matter how you tried to frame the situation, the price for this war would eventually be paid in the form of violent retaliation. Images of children picking up the pieces of family members blown apart by a blast or clinging tearfully to the corpses of their parents became seared in my memory. And when I imagined what those children would do when they grew up, I could not help feeling chilling premonitions alongside my sentiments of pity.

Support for Reconstruction Accelerates in Japan

In January 2002, a conference on aid to Afghanistan was held in Tokyo. The involvement of NGOs became a hot topic in Japan, and throughout the country there arose a groundswell of positive support for Afghan reconstruction. At the conclave, Hamid Karzai, then the chairman of the interim Afghan administration set up with US backing, was joined by foreign ministers or equivalent-level officials from other countries, and decisions were reached regarding the amounts of aid to be provided and other matters. Out of a total aid package of $4.5 billion, Japan was reported to have committed $500 million.

However, there was something unsatisfactory about this event. A certain arrogance was on display among the advanced nations, who seemed to act as if they were bringing civilization to savage tribes under the glittering banner of "Freedom and Democracy." Most notably, the participants ignored how desertification was destroying farm villages within Afghanistan and instead focused on ideas from outside the country. People from the developed world who have grown up in urbanized areas are highly unlikely to have experienced the bitter hardship of famine. It seemed such people thought electricity and telephones were everywhere, and that money would take care of any problems that arose.

As I wrote above, Afghanistan was formerly a self-sufficient agrarian country, and 90 percent of the population were either farmers or nomads. While Afghanis certainly had meager cash incomes, their country was by no means an impoverished one. Food self-sufficiency of course stood at nearly 100 percent (for comparison, the self-sufficiency ratio in grains for Japan is at this writing around 28 percent). That declined as desertification proceeded apace and the amount of arable land contracted to an extreme, and the number of economic refugees mainly from farm villages increased dramatically. To put it simply, the root of the Afghan refugee problem lay in the lack of food to eat. It certainly was not a problem solely caused by the political structure or level of education. What happened was little more than a repeat of the return of Afghan refugees and the rush to provide reconstruction support that had occurred from around 1988 to 1990 upon the withdrawal of the Soviet army. Accordingly, my comments to the Tokyo aid conference were curt. "No matter what, the first thing is to make it possible for people to live. The Afghan problem will likely be forgotten. However, there have been no changes to our plans to date, nor will there be in the future."

The office of the United Nations High Commissioner for Refugees (UNHCR) launched a refugee return program in the spring of 2002 in conjunction with the focus on reconstruction. The program was saddled with enormous difficulties from the start. The agency announced that it would try to repatriate the 2 million refugees who were in Pakistan at a pace of 1 million per year, and the US-backed regime in Kabul promised to guarantee the refugees housing, food, and clothing. The UNHCR announced the following February that 1.4 million of the 2 million refugees—a higher number than expected—had returned home, but subsequent figures eloquently showed the emptiness of this claim. In 2005, the government of Pakistan announced that there were 3 million Afghan refugees in the country. This indicated that over the course of the previous three years, most of the refugees who had gone home had subsequently made a U-turn and returned to Pakistan, along with another 1 million additional refugees. (In 2006, the UNHCR put the number of refugees at 2 million; this would mean that in the end the figure was little changed from 2002.)

Even so, it must be said that the UNHCR's efforts were pointed in the right direction. At the very least, its program was one that considered the issue of keeping people alive. In contrast, most aid groups were concentrated in Kabul alone, and judging from their focus on arguing over the way education should be handled, enforcing gender equality, and so forth, they must have been oblivious to the fact that most people were struggling to get their daily bread.

I am not saying that education and gender equality are superfluous issues. But what of the mother hurrying to the clinic while clutching her desperately ill child, the bewildered housewife who lost her breadwinner husband in a bombing, the farm-village women who travel several kilometers back and forth every day to draw water? I am saying that their voices have not been heard.

THREE

Creating Green Ground
2002–2008

Chapter 5

Seeking to Revive Farm Villages

Closing PMS Clinics in the Backcountry

In June 2002, Peace Japan Medical Services (PMS) closed the five temporary clinics we had been operating in Kabul and firmed up our policy of concentrating on the belt of farm villages located in eastern Afghanistan. However, the rush to provide support for Afghan reconstruction was causing major difficulties. For one thing, there was the spike in prices. Because foreign organizations were liberally spreading their funds around in a market with severely limited supplies, the local economy became awash in money—and nothing but money. The resulting inflation on some items was terrible, with rents rising by a factor of ten or more, and while we foreigners may have been bothered by the higher prices, for already-impoverished locals they were excruciating.

This inflation also affected salaries, causing an exodus of human resources from PMS. In particular, physicians and people with technical skills were attracted by the higher pay that other NGOs offered. Guaranteed salaries in Kabul that were five or even ten times what we could offer, many of them—including not a few of our key physicians—left us, causing a critical shortage in the personnel required to keep our clinics open. This shortage produced an ongoing decline in our medical care activities thereafter.

The greatest psychological blow came when we lost two of the clinics that had been operating in Afghanistan since 1991: the Dara-e-Pech Clinic in Kunar Province and the Wama Clinic in Nuristan Province. Both had been in Afghanistan's utter hinterlands, in places where there were no medical facilities whatsoever. For that very reason, people living in those regions relied on them. But one physician after another had quit and moved to Kabul in search of higher wages. Eighteen had left by December 2004, leaving only four between the two clinics. The situation was the same with senior laboratory technicians. Even though we continued to hire new staff, the younger physicians did not like working in remote rural areas, and they would quit. The shortage of personnel also caused administrative difficulties.

Staffing shortages were not the only problem. The new government's haphazard policies and the military actions of the US and its allies had incalculable negative effects. First, though the idea of expanding medical facilities as part of the reconstruction support effort was a fine one, the implementation of this undertaking through dealings between the NGOs clustered in Kabul and the new government was problematic.

People within the new government were critical of how staff from NGOs, like the personnel of the International Security Assistance Force (ISAF), rarely set foot outside of Kabul. Immediately after the new cabinet was formed in September 2004, the minister overseeing matters related to foreign NGOs suspended the activities of some two thousand of them. Foreign governments, as well as groups with interests at stake, responded negatively to this forceful measure, and perhaps as a consequence the newly appointed minister abruptly resigned. The new regime may indeed have been created with US backing, but up to this point more than 70 percent of the money being handed out for reconstruction support was being channeled through foreign NGOs and organs of the United Nations. Meanwhile, the government in Kabul was hard-pressed to even pay the salaries of its civil servants.

To some degree this was unavoidable, given the lack of progress in setting up government institutions. However, as most aid organizations were focused on distributing grants, and most of their decisions were based on screening paperwork, they were unable to assess practical results. One would assume that if they had sent technical teams that were directly involved with the actual work, the situation would have been vastly improved. This state of affairs had an unfortunate legacy: even after the Afghan government took the lead in decision-making, the poor practice of emphasizing paperwork over substantive activity continued.

In its rush to enhance the country's medical welfare capacity, the government assigned the work in specific regions to foreign NGOs. These assignments were made based on successful bids, and the funding group was to oversee all the medical institutions in the province. Kunar Province, where our Dara-e-Pech clinic was located, was assigned to a private group funded by the European Union: Portugal's Fundação Assistência Médica Internacional (International Medical Assistance Foundation, AMI). Thus, AMI invested in medical facilities throughout Kunar Province, and the PMS clinic was asked to operate under its umbrella in accordance with the new rules that it laid down. However, AMI is not a medical group, but a foundation. Its "new rules"—which simply copied, to a large extent, the operational guidelines used by the United States Agency for International Development (USAID)—stipulated that treatment hours would run from 8 a.m. to noon, that the facility must employ people from the vicinity, and that it had to have a maternity ward. For us, these conditions were unacceptable. We provided treatment from 8 a.m. to 3 p.m. and handled emergency cases even far into the night; following AMI's schedule would have meant curtailing our services. Also, we had been rotating the medical staff between the clinics in Afghanistan and our base hospital in Peshawar on a monthly basis so they could hone their skills while receiving training in Peshawar, and we would not have been able to continue this program under the AMI's new rules. Furthermore, as it was normal in farm villages for childbirth to take place in the home, clinics generally did not need to serve as maternity facilities.

On top of that, the US military was gradually stepping up its Taliban cleanup operations in Kunar and Nuristan provinces, and the military's Civil Affairs unit got involved. Even if foreign aid groups had no ill intentions, it was not unusual for them to be mistakenly seen as part of the US military's efforts to win over the populace. This was substantiated by a series of incidents beginning in autumn 2004 in which personnel from foreign groups were attacked on the streets.

And so, in January 2005, though our clinics in Dara-e-Pech and Wama had managed to carry on despite troubles both locally and back in Japan, we were finally obliged to suspend our services. All of this occurred immediately after we had engaged in new construction and renovations. We knew all too well that, while ostensibly our clinic was simply being handed over to AMI (in essence, to the new government), no medical care worthy of the name would be provided.

When we dispatched our team from Peshawar to the Afghan clinics for the last time, I was reminded of the fifteen years of hard work we had accomplished, and I could not help but feel as though a perfectly healthy tree was being chopped down. I was also filled with inevitable loathing for the heartlessness of the military activities and for the haphazard approach that foreign aid groups were taking. Local residents were sad. Our office in Jalalabad received an endless stream of requests from people asking PMS to reopen its clinics, but all we could tell them was to please wait. Inwardly, I was fuming.

Just barely, thanks to the kindness of government officials in the medical bureaucracy, we were able to hold on to our clinic in Dara-e-Noor, which we continue to operate to this day.

The Drought Continues

Meanwhile, the drought had not abated in the slightest. As described in the previous chapter, PMS had undertaken work on wells in the area around our clinic in Dara-e-Noor and elsewhere after the drought hit in 2000. The number of usable sources of drinking water (mainly wells) in the region as of May 2004 exceeded 1,000. While the number would keep growing, we would still have to dig most of them again because the groundwater would subside. Ultimately, we secured wells for drinking water in about 1,600 locations by 2006, which helped keep more than 200,000 people from having to leave their villages. However, maintaining those wells was a burden; furthermore, as had been the case with our medical activities, our organization was in danger of becoming paralyzed owing to an exodus of technical staff. We had just about reached the limit of what we could do to secure water sources for irrigation use by restoring *karez* (long horizontal wells) and enlarging regular wells. This was because the water had begun to dry up not only near the surface but also deeper in the ground. In the face of the rapidly declining volume of water produced by the *karez*, we dug eleven wells for irrigation use. In this way we managed to revive some one hundred-plus hectares of farmland in parts of Soraj and Budialy villages downstream from Dara-e-Noor. However, this was a rare success. In other areas, there was an endless exodus of people becoming refugees in numbers proportionate to the degree to which desertification had progressed.

The main city in eastern Afghanistan is Jalalabad. It is located in Nangarhar Province, which formerly had been a rich farm belt. The province is flanked by the Keshmand Mountains to the north and the Spin Ghar Mountains to the south, giving it a terrain wedged between the two ranges. The Dara-e-Noor Valley lies on the south side of the Keshmand Mountains. Both of these ranges reach heights of more than 4,000 meters. In the summer, their snowcaps melt, providing the foothills with water. Furthermore, the Kabul River feeds the area from the west, while the Kunar River feeds it from the north. In the past, water drawn from these major rivers had supported this vast rural district, turning it into the largest farm belt in eastern Afghanistan.

The areas that were suffering from the worst drought around this time were the foothills of the Spin Ghar and Keshmand ranges. The snowcaps that had once functioned as enormous water tanks had been shrinking year after year. The summer snowline was now nearly up to 4,000 meters and the snowcaps were on the verge of disappearing. Small amounts of rainfall pushed the water shortage to critical limits. This is not to say that the absolute volumes of rainfall and snowfall had completely dwindled away. In some years, it seemed as though the white snows of days gone by had returned. The problem was the rise in temperatures when spring turned into summer. At this point, the sudden melting of excess snow would produce floods, and in a flash all the snow would be gone.

It is important to understand that the drought did not suddenly occur

Water Circulation, Water Usage, and Causes of Drought in Afghanistan

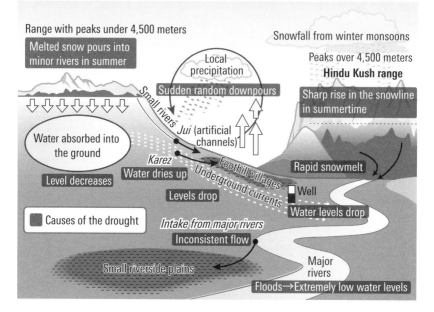

Range with peaks under 4,500 meters

Melted snow pours into minor rivers in summer

Snowfall from winter monsoons

Local precipitation

Peaks over 4,500 meters

Hindu Kush range

Sudden random downpours

Small rivers

Sharp rise in the snowline in summertime

Water absorbed into the ground

Jui (artificial channels)

Level decreases

Karez

Water dries up

Foothill villages

Underground currents

Rapid snowmelt

Levels drop

Well

Water levels drop

Causes of the drought

Intake from major rivers

Inconsistent flow

Small riverside plains

Major rivers

Floods→Extremely low water levels

The lower reaches of the Dara-e-Noor Valley, site of the most severe drought.

Dara-e-Noor Valley

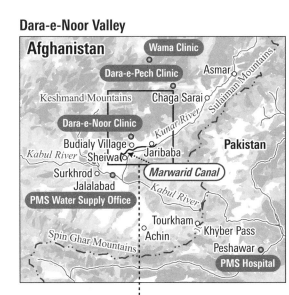

Afghanistan

Wama Clinic

Dara-e-Pech Clinic

Asmar

Sulaiman Mountains

Keshmand Mountains

Chaga Sarai

Kunar River

Dara-e-Noor Clinic

Pakistan

Budialy Village

Kabul River — Sheiwa — Jaribaba

Surkhrod

Marwarid Canal

Jalalabad

PMS Water Supply Office

Kabul River

Tourkham

Achin

Khyber Pass

Spin Ghar Mountains

Peshawar

PMS Hospital

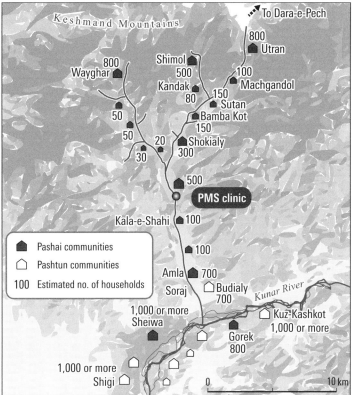

Keshmand Mountains

To Dara-e-Pech

800 Utran

Shimol

800 Wayghar

500

100 Machgandol

Kandak

80

150

50

Sutan

50

Bamba Kot

20

150

30

300 Shokialy

500

PMS clinic

Kala-e-Shahi 100

Pashai communities

Pashtun communities

100 Estimated no. of households

100

Amla 700

Soraj

Budialy
700

Kunar River

1,000 or more
Sheiwa

Kuz-Kashkot
1,000 or more

Gorek
800

1,000 or more
Shigi

0   10 km

in the summer of 2000, when we were just beginning our water-sourcing project. Even in the Himalaya and Karakoram ranges adjacent to the Hindu Kush range, people had observed for years that the snowlines were rising and the glaciers receding.

When PMS opened its clinic in the Dara-e-Noor Valley in 1991, two medium-sized rivers flowed there throughout the year, providing a source of water for the vast farmlands in the plains of that foothills area. Thanks to that water and the intake from the Kunar River, a rich farm belt spread across the northern part of Nangarhar Province. Over the years, however, the flow of water from the Dara-e-Noor Valley dried up. Meanwhile, massive floods that came from the Kunar River in early summer destroyed the intake gates, and as a result agricultural production went into a state of gradual decline. Dealing with climate change, which was producing both flooding and drought conditions, should have been the top priority, but initially this problem failed to attract broad attention.

The "War on Terror" Escalates

It was in this context that the production of opium, which had been almost completely eradicated during the years of Taliban rule, made such a large-scale comeback. On top of the fact that poppy seeds can withstand arid conditions, a cultivator could expect to earn a cash income around a hundred times that obtainable from wheat. Because farmers pinched by the lack of water decided en masse to cultivate poppy seeds, by the end of 2003 Afghanistan as a whole came to account for more than 90 percent of the world's narcotic production. Meanwhile, in Kabul, prostitution targeting foreigners had become rampant, and the numbers of begging widows who had lost their family's breadwinners in the air strikes increased. Thoughtful people were becoming disgusted by the ostentatious lifestyles of foreigners and upper-class Afghans. The contrast between Kabul's luxury hotels and the dilapidated slums that spread out around them was altogether too stark. Conditions had been terrible even before the air strikes, and virtually no improvements had been made since. The Afghan revival seen on television screens in other countries was confined mainly to the one part of the capital where foreigners could easily go back and forth.

Security conditions continued to deteriorate. The US military's efforts to mop up Al Qaeda were fruitless, serving only to stir up anti-American sentiment. In November 2002, anti-American Islamic forces won an overwhelming victory in a general election in Pakistan's North-West Frontier Province.

The PMS crew dug an irrigation well that was 5 meters in diameter at Budialy Village in Dara-e-Noor, but the water level continued to dwindle.

Poppy cultivation saw a resurgence after the collapse of the Taliban regime.

The province's new government publicly denounced the US military and voiced its objections to the operations being conducted along the border with Afghanistan. The fact is, the "mop-up" efforts the foreign forces pursued were crude. They continually bombed mosques and schools by mistake, aggravating people's antagonism and vengeful sentiments. The 12,000-strong US military contingent of 2002 had been increased to 16,000 by 2004 and to 18,000 by 2005. To this, the UK decided to add 4,000 of its own soldiers. (The numbers would continue to increase thereafter, totaling 90,000 by 2008 and swelling to 120,000 by 2010.)

To secure their overland movements, the US forces ratcheted up their helicopter missions. The number of air strikes also increased every year. After a PMS irrigation canal construction site was strafed in November 2003, I protested to the US military authorities, only to be told, "When in doubt, we attack first and check later." They said, "We need you to understand the feelings of fighters who have lost their comrades in combat." I wanted to retort, "We need *you* to understand the feelings of people who have lost relatives in air strikes," but I kept my mouth shut, not wanting to provoke retaliation.

The biggest problem for the US military was their inability to tell the difference between friend and foe. Despite all the calls for "democratization" and for changing laws and driving out the Taliban, it was still not possible to eliminate the cultural breeding ground from which the Taliban had emerged. In 2003, the Northern Alliance—the prime ally of the US forces—took control in Jalalabad. And it was these anti-Taliban forces themselves who revived the laws of the Taliban era, offering the excuse that they were unable to rule under the new laws.

The Decision to Create an Irrigation Canal

Our hearts could not help but ache to see this situation. However, the fickle attention of the world gradually shifted away from Afghanistan, as people accepted the illusion that things there had somehow settled down. They were not aware of the actual situation—that rural residents displaced from their homes around the country were streaming into the big cities, while others were crossing the border and becoming refugees.

I was all the more convinced that Afghanistan would not see a revival if its farm villages did not come back to life. Accordingly, I decided to devote some 600 million yen—money that we had received in response to our pleas for support for food distribution during the bombing—to an all-out effort aimed at reviving farming in the region. The basic plan was as follows.

(1) Pilot farm: Conduct research into crops that can withstand dry conditions.

(2) Drinking-water source project: Maintain operations at the current level and aim to increase the total number of locations to 2,000.

(3) Irrigation project: [1] Build weirs and holding ponds in regions where rivers dry up in the absence of rainfall. [2] Draw in water from a major river; start by building a 13-kilometer-long irrigation canal running from Jaribaba in Kunar Province to the highlands of the Sheiwa district in Nangarhar Province (ultimately, this would be extended to run around 25 kilometers from the intake gate to the far side of the Gamberi Desert).

Dubbing our plan the "Green Ground Project," we quickly began making preparations in March 2002. This project was actually a natural outgrowth of the work of the Jalalabad PMS Water Supply Office that we had launched back in August 2000. The only new element was the pilot farm. Securing water for agricultural purposes was simply an extension of the work we had done up to that point. Be that as it may, building an irrigation canal to provide water for thousands of hectares of land was a project on a greater scale than anything that PMS had undertaken with the support of the Peshawar-kai so far. Moreover, the canal was to go through a region that had been untouched over the three decades since President Daoud's assassination, which had happened when the government's national irrigation project was still in the planning stages.

Nonetheless, our project was not completely reckless. I had quite a good grasp of the topography from Jaribaba—where we planned to build the intake gate from the Kunar River—to Dara-e-Noor. I had traveled through the region numerous times since 1989, when we started making preliminary arrangements for opening clinics in Afghanistan's mountainous regions. Dodging the ongoing fighting, I had shared food and lodging with local guerrilla forces, hidden myself in the mountains, traversed the Sulaiman Mountains on the border with Pakistan, and crossed the great Kunar River by raft more than once.

Aside from a couple of difficult spots, most of the irrigation canals in the area had been excavated without shoring along rock beds. My idea was that we could solve any technical problems with local know-how and achieve our goals with the necessary financing. Given the vast expanses of ruined farmland, the throngs of displaced persons, and the limits on groundwater availability, and knowing that we had around 600 million yen in hand, I believed that we should implement this plan. Thus, the Green Ground Project, to which we devoted our entire store of knowledge and experience, was begun.

I have often said that in Peshawar and Afghanistan we can see all the contradictions of the Asian world. And here, as we grappled with the devastating drought caused by atmospheric warming—the greatest environmental issue of them all—we stood face to face with a fundamental problem that was developing on a global scale.

This challenge was both old and new. I was deeply struck by the words of Tanaka Shōzō, a Japanese politician and social activist who more than a century ago had dedicated his life to solving the problem of pollution from the Ashio copper mine in the watershed of the Watarase River in eastern Japan. He wrote:

Even those poison fields
Are normal wastelands if you look at them without thinking.
If you look only with tears, all you see are the hungry ghosts of hell.
If you look with vital energy, you see a spear.
And if you look in cowardice all you see is disease.

It is vital energy and tears that we lack. PMS, too, would try to manifest the feelings of good-hearted people, turn wastelands green again, and show the vital energy of Japan's better nature.

Chapter 6

Construction of the Irrigation Canal

Starting with Trial and Error

And so the die was cast. On March 19, 2003—the day before the US and UK forces attacked Iraq—we brought together senior officials of the local government, members of the Sheiwa district council of elders, and representatives of Peace Japan Medical Services (PMS) to hold a groundbreaking ceremony. We declared that within a few years' time we would build an irrigation canal that stretched about 13 kilometers from Jaribaba, and with this we would be able to restore 3,000 hectares in the Sheiwa district that had turned into desert. The canal, which was to be named "Aab-e-Marwarid" (Water of Pearl), would deliver 6 tons of water per second (500,000 tons per day) to the drought-stricken region. There was no stepping back after this.

However, I cannot say that we possessed the abilities required for living up to our declaration. I had the Japanese workers who were to be involved with the canal project read *Kōsei e no saidai ibutsu* (The greatest legacy) by Uchimura Kanzō and *Nihon no kome* (Rice in Japan) by environmental affairs commentator and scholar Tomiyama Kazuko. Basically, all we had was the audacity to take on the challenge. As for myself, I could not understand books about flow-rate calculations and fluid channel design. I borrowed textbooks from my high-school-aged daughter and set about relearning mathematics, which I was never good at in the first place. Two specialists in riparian engineering who helped me at this time without laughing were Professor Sakamoto Kōji of Kyushu University and the engineer Kobayashi Masaki. Our public relations officer Fukumoto Mitsuji (who went on to become manager of the Peshawar-kai administrative office) bustled about and created opportunities for me to learn.

I learned the basics of how to pour foundational concrete, as well as how to work with cement and assemble rebar. In fact, I also visited construction sites in Japan. I was starting almost from scratch. Looking back now, it strikes me that the job I decided to undertake was one that no professional engineer would have touched. However, it did not seem to me that a Japanese civil engineer would be useful right away. With materials and mechanical power

Marwarid Canal, Phase One

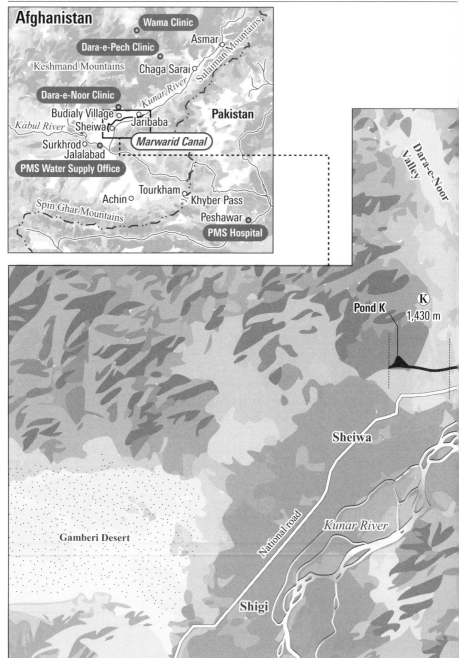

Afghanistan
Wama Clinic
Asmar
Dara-e-Pech Clinic
Keshmand Mountains
Chaga Sarai
Kunar River
Sulaiman Mountains
Pakistan
Dara-e-Noor Clinic
Budialy Village
Kabul River
Sheiwa
Jaribaba
Marwarid Canal
Surkhrod
Jalalabad
PMS Water Supply Office
Tourkham
Achin
Khyber Pass
Spin Ghar Mountains
Peshawar
PMS Hospital

Dara-e-Noor Valley
Pond K
(K) 1,430 m
Sheiwa
National road
Kunar River
Gamberi Desert
Shigi

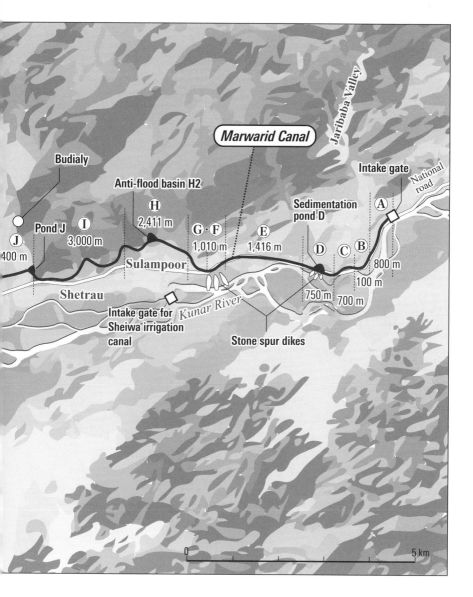

Marwarid Canal

Jaribaba Valley

Budialy

Anti-flood basin H2

Ⓗ
2,411 m

Intake gate

National road

Sedimentation pond D

Ⓐ

Pond J

Ⓘ
3,000 m

Ⓖ·Ⓕ
1,010 m

Ⓔ
1,416 m

Ⓓ Ⓒ Ⓑ

Ⓙ
400 m

800 m

100 m

Sulampoor

Shetrau

750 m   700 m

Intake gate for
Sheiwa irrigation
canal

Kunar River

Stone spur dikes

0   5 km

available in tremendous amounts and the capacity to make precision surveys and conduct theoretical research, Japan's civil engineering technologies and techniques are among the best in the world. This is reflected in the extreme specialization of the field, which leaves little room for an outsider to get involved. In this respect it is not unlike the realm of medical technology in Japan. In that field, even if a technician is superb, their skills are supported by a social welfare system that provides them with an abundance of diagnostic equipment and the necessary medications. Few such specialists would even be able to conduct an examination if they had to rely solely on their senses and basic equipment like a stethoscope and reflex hammer.

As for agricultural techniques and small water-use facilities, farmers with skills honed by self-sufficiency were much quicker on the uptake than any engineer who grew up in an urban environment. You cannot put food on the table with desktop theories. However, with a physician like myself leading the project, a process of trial and error was inevitable. As with the medical care we provided locally, our goals were to avoid relying excessively on modern mechanical power or technology, to aim for work that the local farmers could do, and to make it possible for them to handle maintenance and repairs. The only work on irrigation facilities that I undertook myself was the repair of a minor *karez* (lateral well)—not something you could describe as a "waterway."

Applying Techniques from Japan's Past

Both in Afghanistan and when I had free time on trips back to Japan, I would walk around looking at water-use facilities. Starting with streams and reservoirs in the vicinity, I set my sights on places that had been around for a long time. My strolls took me along the Chikugo and Yabe rivers in Fukuoka Prefecture, and along the Kikuchi, Midori, and Kuma rivers in Kumamoto Prefecture. I wanted to see from places close at hand just how my Japanese ancestors had gotten water from rivers, how they had created artificial waterways, and how they were able to bring so much land under cultivation. Of course, there were many irrigation channels and intake structures in Afghanistan as well, and people were making lives for themselves there, so I also studied the local water-use facilities. However, they had taken just about all the water they could get from available sources, and now they were struggling with drought. Unless some new twists could be added to their local approach, they would probably have no real future in sight. The techniques they had been using for drawing water were inadequate for keeping up with climate change.

As a result of my observations, a new world opened before my eyes. The sight of the fields I had gazed at unthinkingly until then changed completely. People can see only what they try to see. How did our forebears gauge the incline of the seemingly level Chikugo Plain in Kyushu and determine how much water would be needed to irrigate it? How did they decide on the route for sending water along, and did they adjust volumes from season to season? When I saw rice paddies and rivers through the window as I was traveling, I would take in everything before my eyes and think about it.

My house is near the border between Fukuoka and Kumamoto prefectures, in a hilly part of the Miike district of the city of Ōmuta. If you go about 500 meters along a path through the woods you will be in Nankan, a town in Kumamoto that has a different riverine system. Previously, I had never thought about how they determined the border between the two prefectures, but now I understood. Naturally, it was because the village communities were located on different riverine systems.

Also, the area around my house is at an elevation of about 40 meters. From there you can see right across the Sea of Ariake to the Shimabara Peninsula in Nagasaki Prefecture. There are many terraced fields, and no large rivers. Instead there are holding ponds all over the place—eleven just within a 500-meter radius of my house. They say that because Miike has no large rivers, since ancient times people living here would store water during the rainy season and release it during the dry times of summer and autumn.

It is not unusual to find old stone monuments at these reservoirs, from which we can see that countless generations of villagers had done the work of maintaining them themselves. The monuments list the names of the people who participated in construction and repair work up to the 1930s or so, and they always include messages of thanks along the lines of "Large numbers of people from village X volunteered to help with the construction." The foundations for a lasting agricultural lifestyle could not be sustained without the villagers pulling together. Afghanistan today is the same in that the dredging of major waterways and the maintenance work on water gates are handled by all the villagers.

Japan and Afghanistan seem at a glance to be extremely different countries. But as I learned more about irrigation, I came to see connections between the two. I also noted similarities between their rivers and their farming environments. For one thing, both have many fast-flowing rivers in the mountains. For another, there are considerable differences in water levels between winter and spring. Still another similarity is that, apart from few large plains, farming is carried out in basins and small plateaus sandwiched between mountains. This is a point of difference with the countries of Europe and North America, which have stretches of great plains. Johannis de Rijke, a Dutch civil engineer invited to come to Japan during the 1870s, is famously said to have remarked upon seeing a Japanese river: "That's not a river—that's a waterfall!"

Japan's wet season is produced by the seasonal rain front that generally forms over most of the country for a period starting in June and extending well into July, along with the typhoons that pass through the area from summer through early fall. Floods are a common occurrence in the summer. However, the forests that cover the Japanese archipelago play a major role, storing enormous amounts of water and stabilizing the volume of rivers. This is the reason why waters flow in the rivers through all four seasons and the groundwater remains constant.

In Afghanistan, the Asian monsoons of winter produce rain and snow in the Hindu Kush mountain range. Much of the summer rainfall takes the form of localized, concentrated downpours and hence is unstable. The snowfall replenishes the snowcaps on the taller mountains, and in the summer the thaw and runoff from these stabilize the volume of water in the rivers. There are no forests like those in Japan, but the snowcaps play a similar role, functioning as an enormous water tank.

Designing Intake Gates

In the mountainous regions of the Afghan backcountry, the artificial channels called *jui* are a frequent sight. Traveling around the valleys in the Hindu Kush and Karakoram mountain ranges, one can see how the small communities next to rocky deserts and Indus River tributaries must struggle to draw water. The *jui* are what keep these human habitations barely hydrated. Generally drawing water from springs and the upper reaches of rivers, they crawl along the mountainside for several kilometers. The larger channels that can be seen around communities on the plains relatively close to a river are basically the same as the *jui*, differing from them only in scale.

The villages located along rivers in the mountainous areas could be compared to desert oases. I had long wondered why people drew water to such distant places, but when I looked at it from the perspective of the people who obtained and used that water, I understood it for the first time. The fast-flowing major tributaries of the Indus River are both a blessing and at the same time a source of fear for people. In the case of the Kunar River, the difference in water levels between summer and winter was 1.5 meters or more at its widest sections and 2.5 meters or more at its narrowest. It is safe to assume that major floods occur along it every year. At locations that are slightly lower in elevation, if the water levels rise even a bit too much in the summer, the

The work of digging up the parched soil for an irrigation canal begins.

Construction of the irrigation canal was accomplished by putting large numbers of people to work.

turbid waters can easily overcome inhabited areas, making them unlivable. I learned that, just as in Japan, people had over the years come up with various contrivances for obtaining water while doing battle with flooding.

Naan flatbread, the staple local food, is made using wheat raised in the winter. Accordingly, drawing water is important in this season. However, if the intake gates are too big and too deep, residents will have to worry about floods in the summer. Also, the turbid summer flow of the Kunar River, which is fed by water from melting snow, carries with it particles of earth and sand of various sizes from tributary areas. When the summer downpours are mixed in, the entire surface of the river turns into something that might better be described as a muddy colloid than as water. The sediment builds up as the water enters the flow channel, making the waterway shallower.

The buildup of sediment is especially heavy in the parts of the river close to the irrigation water gates, and a considerable portion of the work of farming involves dredging to clear it away. When the water levels start to subside in autumn, several hundred men from the villages pick up their shovels every day and dredge the sediment near the water gates. For this reason, the farmers long for clear water. If they could reduce the effort spent on dredging, they would be able to get that much more work done in the fields.

Although Japan's rivers are not as muddy as Afghanistan's, people there were nonetheless confronted with the same sort of problem, and the techniques for drawing clear water from rivers and ponds were used throughout Japan. Before the introduction of concrete, most of the intake gates for reservoirs consisted of barriers made of removable flashboards set on top of one another to hold the water back. These were useful for adjusting the volume of water being supplied. And since muddy water is heavier than clear water, it naturally tends to sink, so by removing the flashboards one at a time starting at the top, the water flowing over can be kept relatively free of mud. It is not known exactly how this use of flashboards originated, but thanks in part to the abundance of wood, the method became widespread throughout Japan.

Of course, the use of flashboards alone is not enough to provide a supply of clear water. Another key consideration is how to determine the height of the barrier required in order to draw a specific amount of water. Suddenly intake gate research and design was the first bit of homework assigned to me, and it became a major undertaking up to the end.

The Oblique Weir: The Wisdom and Great Work of Our Forebears

In the city of Asakura, in Fukuoka Prefecture, there is an intake gate known as the Yamada Weir. Oblique weirs apparently were once seen all around Japan, but this is the only one still in its original state. It is located in the basin of the Chikugo River, a major waterway with a watershed whose area accounts for one-third of the total in Kyushu. It provides water for the Chikugo Plain, which is Kyushu's grain-producing region. The Chikugo is said to be one of Japan's three wildest (i.e., most likely to flood) rivers, along with the Tone in the Kantō region and the Yoshino in Shikoku. Due to these similarities, I thought we might find things here that could be applied to the Kunar River in Afghanistan.

There was a time when I could have gazed out a car or train window at the vast expanse of rice paddies and just soaked up the pastoral setting. But now the scene brought practical questions to my mind: Where is the water source that irrigates all those paddies? How is the water drawn in? How have they prevented floods? How did they expand the area being irrigated, taking the gradient into account?

At one point, I was looking at a map and happened to notice a place where the intake gates and terrain closely resembled that seen on the Kunar; namely, the Yamada Weir on the Chikugo River. At Jaribaba, which was to be the starting place for our Marwarid Canal, the running water blocked by solid bedrock on the right bank spread across the width of the Kunar toward the left bank and formed a small cove that curved away from the river like a snail's shell. Large boulders strewn about the riverbed in this cove-like place formed a sort of carpet, and a sedimented sandy beach stretched along the downstream side.

The two places resembled one another so closely on the map that I went to have a look in person. Sure enough, at the Yamada Weir bedrock also protruded from the right bank. It repelled water and was the same sort of terrain. The solid bedrock would not budge one bit even in a flood, and the running water created the same sort of snail-shaped pattern in the river as it bounced back to the left bank.

The intake gate had been created by boring into this bedrock. The water was drawn in by a type of irrigation canal called a *horikawa*. Built in 1663, this *horikawa* provided enough water to irrigate 660 hectares of fertile paddy. Records show that the work of boring through the bedrock took place in 1722, and that major repairs to the weir used to maintain the water at a specific level were performed in 1790. The weir was 120 meters wide and 240

The Yamada Weir on the Chikugo River.

An oblique weir created on the Kunar River.

meters long. Great boulders lined up at an angle across the river blocked the current, causing the water level to rise several meters. Two boat channels and one sand-flushing ditch were provided to keep the water level steady when the river swelled during the winter. When even vaster increases occurred in the summer, the spillage would run across the top of the weir. Nowadays, of course, barriers can be created by using concrete to bind smaller stones together, but in the era when this weir was created, these immense rocks had to be transported by raft, ox, and horse and then lined up without the help of any heavy machinery. As I imagined this feat, I was more than amazed; indeed, I was struck by a sense of awe.

My encounter with the Yamada Weir led to the introduction of techniques and technologies that would play a crucial role in the revival of the grain-producing regions in northern Jalalabad. I will touch on this point in more detail later. At first, I was bent on making a copy of that weir, but every year we made improvements, and the project drew closer to completion.

The Beauty of Nature: Reading Water

As we launched our project, there was no avoiding the fact that we lacked mechanical power and material resources. It seemed that it would take six months to procure a single excavator. Furthermore, getting materials and equipment over to the opposite shore required a trip of 20 kilometers down the meandering river to cross a bridge and then traveling some 20 kilometers up bad roads on the other side. We were compelled to do our construction work from only the right bank.

However, our lack of material resources and technology served as one way to open our eyes. Afghan farm villages are basically self-sufficient and are strongly disposed toward autonomy. Unlike in Japan, Afghanistan's central government has done little to maintain irrigation facilities throughout the country. Most of the maintenance and repair work done on the intake gates and irrigation channels is handled by the villagers themselves. In short, it would be useless to construct something that the locals could not subsequently repair themselves. Creating something that would be costly to repair was also out of the question.

In Japan until recently it was exceedingly common to line waterways with concrete, but this approach has been reconsidered. At a 2003 meeting of a government council on riparian affairs, recommendations were made related to biodiversity and the reassessment of traditional technologies. On small and medium rivers, we started to see the revival of gabions, brush mattresses, and willow revetments. Of these, viewed in terms of what we could build on site, the gabion technique was far and away the easiest technologically and would also be the easiest to maintain and repair.

Gabions are large wire baskets filled with rocks used to reinforce waterway embankments. They have the following advantages:

(1) They do not crack.
(2) They can be freely enlarged or shrunk.
(3) If broken, they can be repaired by anyone with a basket and rocks.
(4) Vegetation adapts to them, and they are a habitat for other living things.
(5) They are not too costly.

Embankments made with gabions become even sturdier when combined with live-willow revetments. Willow trees grown behind the gabions extend countless roots into the cracks between the rocks and create a "living basket." The willow is a marvelous plant. No matter how thick its trunk becomes, it will not knock over solid objects, and even if submerged, its roots do not rot.

We therefore mainly used gabions and willow trees to line the banks of our irrigation canal. On site, we needed no professional stonemasons. The farmers we employed to work on the project were all competent stonemasons themselves. They used stone on a regular basis to create the boundaries for their fields, to lay the foundations for their houses, and to build walls. They also built comfortable homes from mud and stone. And there was an abundance of stone available for next to nothing. PMS built its own workshop to produce gabions. From 2003 to 2010, we used 500 tons of wire to produce tens of thousands of gabions. The people we hired for this work were also farmers, and they have since become what we may well call skilled workers.

Obtaining Clean Water

The flashboard method for getting clean water from rivers was itself revolutionary for Afghanistan. Using this, you could keep sediment in the muddy summer waters down to just some grains of sand and bits of earth that would float to the top. Still, it was impossible to clean it completely, and the water at our intake to the canal from the Kunar was still muddy. We therefore arranged for it to flow down a slope in a rapid current for an additional 1.6 kilometers, after which it would come to rest in a sedimentation pond 350 meters in diameter; it would then run again through a flashboard-type floodgate at the

Basic Diagram of Gabion and Willow Techniques Used in Area A

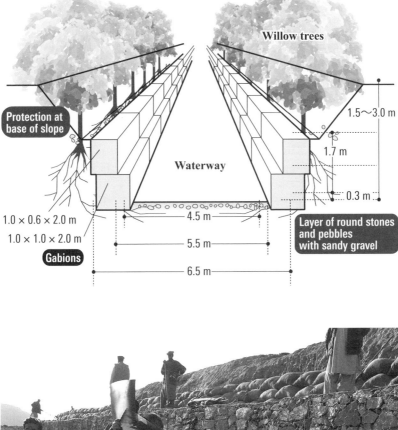

Willow trees

Protection at base of slope

Waterway

1.5～3.0 m

1.7 m

0.3 m

1.0 × 0.6 × 2.0 m

1.0 × 1.0 × 2.0 m

Gabions

4.5 m

5.5 m

6.5 m

Layer of round stones and pebbles with sandy gravel

Embankment on the irrigation canal made using the gabion technique.

exit from the pond. The sediment settled around the entrance to the pond, and the water from near the surface that passed through the flood gate at the exit was surprisingly clear.

After monitoring the sedimentation pond for two years and seeing that it was still functioning, we concluded it would probably be sufficient to do a dredging operation once every few years. I got the idea of running the water down a slope from a Japanese model, a distinctive waterway known as the Hanaguri Ide constructed in the early 1600s. Placed in the upper reaches of the Shirakawa River in today's Kumamoto Prefecture, it was designed so that water flowing through it would be stirred up to prevent volcanic ash in it from settling and accumulating on the bottom of the waterway.

Construction of the sedimentation pond began in April 2004 and took ten months to complete. No one had ever built a reservoir on this scale in Afghanistan before, but we proved that it was possible to store water with this way even in a region where snowfall had decreased. Later, we would build twelve reservoirs of varying sizes at places along the irrigation canal. The largest of these was "Reservoir Q2" at the irrigation canal's 20-kilometer point. It measured 360 meters across along its major axis, 180 meters on its minor axis, and could hold 200,000 cubic meters of water. For the design, I drew on the model of the reservoirs we are familiar with in Japan, referring to the ones seen around my home.

Greenery Comes Back to Life

I will skip the details of subsequent difficulties that arose and how we dealt with them. We went through seven years truly on only spirit and willpower. Natural disasters in the form of great floods and concentrated local downpours on a scale not seen for several centuries were not the only problems. We also faced human-caused troubles, such as mistaken attacks on the wrong targets by US forces, sabotage by local warlords, anti-American violence, desertions by engineers, betrayals, robberies, malfeasance by staff, internal conflicts, struggles with people living on the opposite bank, disputes with landholders about acquiring the land to be used—the list was endless. On a personal level, I lost numerous relatives and friends, had to leave my family behind, and failed to fulfill various obligations. These things caused my spirits to ebb at times. Under conditions that felt desperate, I even felt tempted to abandon the canal and end my own life. To be honest, hand-to-hand combat on the battlefield might have been easier. I set aside my pride to accomplish the task. It was like walking a tightrope, but somehow I managed to surmount the crises. When I considered the vast sums of money we were using,

Basic Principles of the Sedimentation Pond

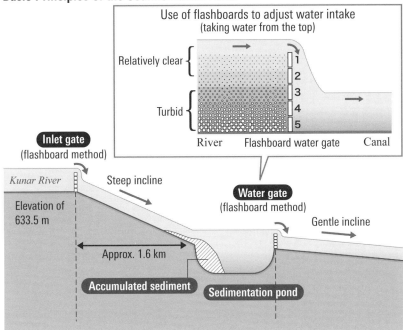

Use of flashboards to adjust water intake
(taking water from the top)

Relatively clear

Turbid

1
2
3
4
5

River　　Flashboard water gate　　Canal

Inlet gate
(flashboard method)

Kunar River

Steep incline

Elevation of
633.5 m

Water gate
(flashboard method)

Gentle incline

Approx. 1.6 km

Accumulated sediment

Sedimentation pond

The outlet gate at sedimentation pond D.

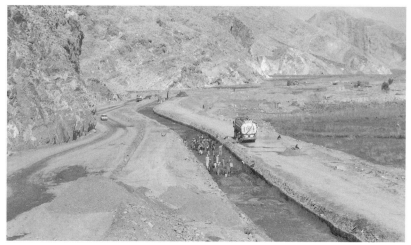

Area FG, with excavation underway on the waterway, in 2005.

The same area seven years after beginning irrigation. (July 2012.)

the hopes we had stirred up in many people's hearts, and the countless starving refugees who were thirsting for water, I could not complain.

Meanwhile, in Japan, even though Afghanistan had slipped from most people's minds, we were still raising 300 million yen a year thanks to the great efforts of the Peshawar-kai. And we had an estimated 20,000 donating members. I have to particularly stress that our irrigation canal project, alongside our provision of medical services, would have been impossible without the benevolent, charitable cooperation of these donors.

The Sulampoor district before irrigation in 2005.

The same area seven years after beginning irrigation. (August 2012.)

In April 2005, we broke through the area of bedrock at the 4.5-kilometer point (Area FG) that had presented the biggest hurdle, and our first target—the broad, flat expanse of Sulampoor—came into view. The 20-meter drop from the Kunar River to the waterway below made it easy to send the water along. Thus, the irrigation of 480 hectares that had been our first objective began.

Almost right away, houses began to appear in what had been an uninhabited wasteland, and villages and green fields that had disappeared twenty years or more before suddenly reappeared. It was neither dream nor mirage.

The refugees returned with a real sense of safety. And with the completion of the first phase of the project at 13 kilometers in April 2007, we had revived a broad expanse of farmland that measured more than 1,200 hectares. The area was blanketed in green to such an extent that it was difficult to find traces of its previous desertification.

Madrassa and Mosque Construction

Building an irrigation canal certainly created a lifeline for local residents. However, just providing a supply of water was not enough. Maintaining the irrigation system was not going to be possible without the cooperation of the village communities that were coming back to life around it. The number of people returning to resume farming in the irrigation canal watershed increased, but during the long period of their absence the social order had frayed.

A distinctive feature of Afghan villages is that, while each is independent, they maintain order among themselves on the basis of Islam and the unwritten code that they share. The elders from each village association gather together every Friday to pray at the main mosque of their region, and most local disputes are resolved there. Large mosques normally operate madrassas, which are traditional schools that serve as the core of the local education system. These schools do not just teach Islam, but also provide education in general subjects such as mathematics and English. Devout farmers are more likely to send their children to a madrassa than to a public school, and even orphans and children from poor families are given the opportunity to learn there.

This previously deserted area, however, had neither mosque nor madrassa. A space had been set aside for their construction, but no work had even begun. The lot was right at the end point of construction for phase one. We asked locals about the matter, and they said that while everyone was eager to have a mosque and a madrassa, no one was doing anything about it.

This was a time when people around the world saw madrassas as hotbeds of extreme Islamic fundamentalism and therefore of the Taliban, and so madrassas and mosques were being bombed regularly. Many feared that if they were built here, they could be taken to show the presence of anti-US elements and invite similar attacks. From our perspective, however, having these facilities was indispensable to the lives of the farmers. We spoke to the education minister for the province, and he was of the same view: "Large mosques and madrassas are essential to the community, but getting foreigners to understand this is difficult."

In February 2007, as phase one of the irrigation canal construction work was coming to an end, PMS began work on building a mosque and a madrassa

The mosque (left) and madrassa under construction.

The completed mosque and madrassa in 2013. The irrigation canal runs in the foreground.

The completed mosque.

Children play in the courtyard of the madrassa.

in response to residents' wishes. We did the design and construction ourselves, incorporating Afghan styles. A national-level religious council also got involved, and the undertaking was reported as a major development. It was impressive to hear the shouts of the people at the groundbreaking ceremony: "We've been liberated!" they cheered. "With this, we've become free!" The work was completed in 2010. The mosque has space for 1,200 to come and pray, and 600 children are attending the madrassa.

To these people, who had been denied their traditional culture, having a mosque and madrassa was comparable to having water in terms of being given back a foundation for their lives. Shrines in Japan might be an apt point of comparison. In the past, shrines and temples were central as sites for local festivals and for offering prayers for rain. In Afghanistan, these facilities are not "cultural assets" from the past—even today, they are part of a living, breathing culture.

As Mencius put it, "Good timing, geographical convenience, and harmonious relations among people" are crucial for success. Applying that to the irrigation canal project meant getting a good read on the region's natural conditions, showing respect for local culture, and having people work harmoniously together. This sums up our major guiding principles.

To the Gamberi Desert

With this, our work on the irrigation canal entered the next stage. Phase two was now the topic of discussion, with our goal being to revive the entire Sheiwa district (approximately 3,500 hectares).

Our initial plan seemed like a dream: If we could extend the canal about 10 more kilometers, we would be able to restore another 2,000 hectares and on top of that raise the possibility of creating an enormous area of reclaimed land in the unpopulated Gamberi Desert. The entire section where construction was to take place ran along foothills of bedrock. The work was expected to be difficult. At the same time, because we would be moving forward while also doing repairs on the already-constructed section, the work would be on an even grander scale.

However, by this time a hundred members of our staff and around five hundred of our workers had learned the techniques for irrigation canal construction. Producing and assembling clay pipe and gabions, planting trees, blasting, excavating bedrock, extracting and transporting stone, surveying—they had a grasp of basically all the techniques necessary for building an irrigation canal, and they had become more efficient at their jobs. We had

Siphons

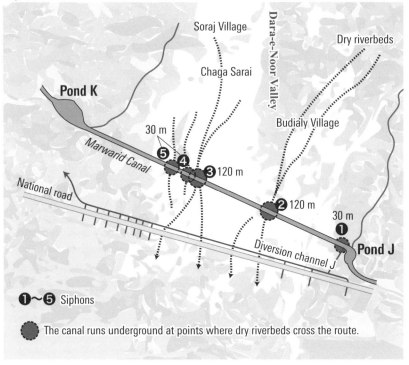

Soraj Village

Dara-e-Noor Valley

Chaga Sarai

Dry riverbeds

Pond K

30 m

Budialy Village

❺ ❹ ❸ 120 m

Marwarid Canal

❷ 120 m

National road

30 m

❶

Diversion channel J

Pond J

❶~❺ Siphons

The canal runs underground at points where dry riverbeds cross the route.

Siphon cross-section

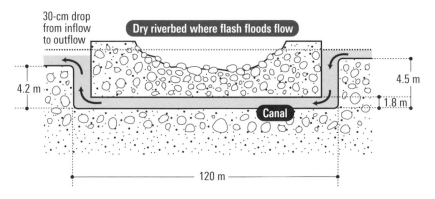

30-cm drop from inflow to outflow

Dry riverbed where flash floods flow

4.2 m

4.5 m

1.8 m

Canal

120 m

Stone spur dikes

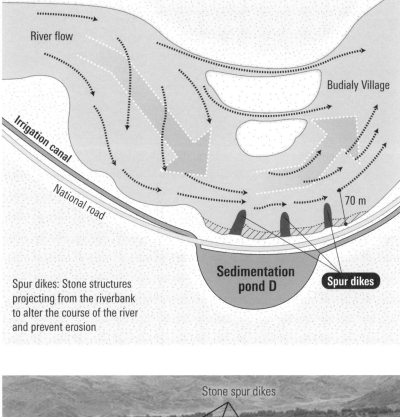

River flow

Budialy Village

Irrigation canal

National road

70 m

Spur dikes: Stone structures
projecting from the riverbank
to alter the course of the river
and prevent erosion

**Sedimentation
pond D**

Spur dikes

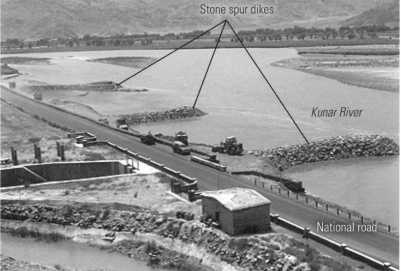

Stone spur dikes

Kunar River

National road

settled on specific styles and procedures for building the concrete structures—bridges, siphons, flood gates, aqueducts, and so forth—essential to the canal, and we had trained a corps of skilled workers. We also became able to mobilize heavy machinery in force, using workers able at the very least to handle dump trucks, power shovels, loaders, and jackhammers, and these operators rapidly achieved proficiency.

As before, the river works accounted for the largest part of our budget. But in light of the other demands on our organization, deciding where to put those resources was always a struggle. Given those limitations, after some trial and error we came up with a "PMS method" for construction of the embankments and weirs. For the embankments, we would build a continuous levee using a combination of spur dikes, open levees, and tree planting, while for the weirs it had become technically possible to do work on the opposite shore and raise the river channel as a whole. For these tasks, while we had a lot of leeway to rely on the skills of our equipment operators, we also received considerable assistance from the company that rented us the heavy equipment and so were able to mobilize a steady workforce.

Chapter 7

Relocating Our Base Hospital and Evacuating Japanese Staff

The Evacuation Plan

The number of Japanese workers increased when construction on the irrigation canal began. Previously, we had limited ourselves to bringing in medical staff. However, we started needing people who could help with farming and civil engineering. This opened the door to bringing in more volunteers from Japan. At any given time we would have twenty Japanese workers altogether. They normally stayed for a term of one to two years, with some extending it to four or five years. By 2008, a cumulative total of around fifty people had come to work in Afghanistan. The majority were in their twenties, and while it was hard for them to be suddenly tossed into a foreign culture, within six months they would acquire enough Pashto to engage in everyday conversation and gradually get acclimated. Their presence was a major support for our work. However, they also faced dangers.

At the time, more than 80 percent of the goods brought into Afghanistan came from Pakistan by way of the Khyber Pass. This was also a major supply route for the forces from the North Atlantic Treaty Organization (NATO) countries. Convoys of vehicles transporting goods were frequently attacked, and keeping the supply lines open was a headache for the Western forces.

For that reason, NATO forces sought help from the Pakistani government. Pakistani forces assisted in the "War on Terror" along the border areas, but their effectiveness was debatable. During the early years of the war, Pakistan's president was Pervez Musharraf. The Taliban regime had diplomatic relations with only Pakistan and Saudi Arabia, and had embassies in each. When the terrorist attacks of September 11, 2001, happened in New York and Washington, DC, the US stepped up its pressure. The Pakistani authorities arrested Afghanistan's ambassador to their country, Abdul Salam Zaeef. This made it plain that they were cooperating with the war effort. (Musharraf would later speak of his humiliation at Washington's threat to bomb his country "back to the Stone Age" if they did not do so.)

The Pakistan-Afghanistan border had its origins in the Durand Line. This was established in 1893 through a treaty agreement between British India and the

Emirate of Afghanistan that turned the latter into a buffer zone between British and Russian interests in the region. However, because this line divided the Pashtun homeland between two countries, it was not a logical choice for a border.

People in eastern Afghanistan usually think of both Kabul and Peshawar as their capital cities, and they move freely back and forth across the border. The common currency here is the Pakistan rupee. It is not unusual for people to have family on both sides of the border. The idea of drawing an international border here was an attempt to do the impossible. It is as if Japan were to be divided in two, with Tokyo and Kyoto belonging to different countries. The older people here take pride in their forebears' having driven back the British in the three Anglo-Afghan wars (of 1838, 1878, and 1919), and anti-British and anti-US sentiment runs strong on both sides of the line. Pakistan's government established an autonomous region along the border and adopted a policy that granted residents the right to cross the border at will; it left the situation ambiguous, treating the area as a kind of buffer zone. Historically, it was rare for Pakistan's army to enter the autonomous region, and if it did, it would inevitably encounter local resistance. Naturally, Pakistan's participation in the "War on Terror" petered out.

There was no clear cause for concern over this at the time. Foreign news broadcasts were talking about the "steady pace of recovery" and the sporadic guerrilla attacks that occurred tended to be ineffectual in the face of the increasingly overwhelming power of the NATO forces. I had no special sources of inside information. However, intuiting popular sentiment from casual conversations with local workers and villagers, and connecting that with the Afghanistan-related news passed on to us by Sawada Yuko, who had previously been working with us in-country, I had a general grasp of the developments. While an outsider might not be aware of what was going on, if you were local you heard enough to know who stood where.

The foreign media's reportage about Afghanistan is limited by the fact that their reporters' contacts are mainly people of the relatively Westernized classes in the big cities, prominent political leaders, and military sources. They have few opportunities to get a sense of what the silent, poorest segment of the population is feeling. Even if they could manage to interview such people, there would be no guarantee that they were being told what the speaker really felt. This is not a conflict where it is easy to clearly divide the parties involved into two sides; i.e., the government and its NATO supporters versus the anti-government forces of Taliban. The situation is considerably more complex. There are regional and blood ties, conflicts among tribes and ethnic groups, and on top of that the tangle of behind-the-scenes maneuvering by intelligence services.

Some of the Japanese workers who gave their all in Afghanistan.

After a series of developments that took place below the surface, I surmised that some sort of chaos on a grand scale was close at hand. Fearing a political avalanche, in March 2008 I decided to send our Japanese workers back home. There had been sporadic violence and assassinations earlier, but this time it felt as though the situation was getting out of control. There was no helping the fact that it generally took time for newly arrived Japanese staff to become sensitized to local security concerns and aware of how their behavior came across to people operating in a different culture. This was a particular problem when they were in groups, and many times their interactions left me in a cold sweat. For that reason, I kept a sharp eye on them, especially at work sites, and counseled them so they would become accustomed to local conditions.

Most farm villages at the time were home to the armed insurgents who supported the former Taliban regime. However one may judge the Taliban, the fact is that many of them were what you might call Afghan ultranationalists. They were wary of the spread of Western culture and considered their own cultural values extremely important. Such an attitude was not exclusive to the Taliban—conservative farmers in general tended to feel this way. In Japan, the news about Afghanistan was generally based on Western sources, and it was not unusual during the anti-Taliban campaign for such reporting to be critical of Islam and Afghan customs. When I conveyed my own perceptions to people in Japan, I was surprised at times to be taken for a Taliban sympathizer.

In any case, even traversing the Tourkham border crossing had become difficult, and rotating twenty Japanese workers was also becoming risky. I felt that protecting this large a group was getting beyond the limits of what I could do personally. But they were all surprised when, late in March, I told them of my decision to pull them out. Their work seemed to be going smoothly, and they were enjoying shopping in the bazaars with no sense of danger. They all seemed to think, "And this, after I've finally gotten used to living here." Some expressed their displeasure with the grudging tone of their words of acceptance. When office manager Serisawa Seiji and six staff members returned to Japan on vacation, I told them to remain there. One of our staffers had become strongly attached to Afghanistan and was reluctant to leave.

Speaking to the workers about the pullout plan, I said, "No matter how long you stay, at some point the day of return must come. I can't thank you enough for your extraordinary efforts. But if you care about this place, I'd like you to set your own feelings aside and cooperate [with the pullout]."

That was all I could say. We selected Afghans from each group to take over operations, and the Japanese were to give them technical guidance for a brief time before going home. The last of our Japanese workers were to be pulled out by December 2008 at the latest. The problem was our agriculture team, who were half settled in at our pilot farm in Dara-e-Noor. After I informed him of the pullout plans, Takahashi Osamu, who was leading the team from Japan, began looking into preparations for withdrawing. But the situation was changing drastically. I was surprised to hear that Takahashi had already issued detailed instructions for everything up to the winter farm work. Chaos was imminent, and I asked the Japan office to stop soliciting for more workers. The dispatch of the Self-Defense Forces that happened around that time further increased the sense of impending crisis.

There were three Japanese workers stationed at the clinic in Dara-e-Noor: Itō Kazuya and Shindō Yōichirō of the agriculture support team and Nishino Kyōhei of the medical team. Transportation was poor at the time. They were rarely able to make it to Jalalabad for our regular meetings, and they tended to fall out of contact. However, the Peace Japan Medical Services (PMS) clinic had been operating since 1991, and over those sixteen years the local community had come to depend on it greatly. Furthermore, these three men had given the villagers a good impression by quietly blending into the local community and taking the lead in tackling hard jobs. They had done so well, in fact, that I had directed staff to take refuge at the Dara-e-Noor clinic if a disturbance occurred in Jalalabad in my absence. But this very success backfired. The Japanese clinic workers were simply not careful enough, and believed that they would be accepted in the same way wherever they were in Afghanistan.

Itō's Abduction

On August 26, 2008, Itō was abducted on his way to our pilot farm at Budialy Village in the Dara-e-Noor Valley. His body was discovered the following day. The story was widely reported in the Japanese media. Emperor Akihito and Empress Michiko heard the news and indirectly paid their respects by canceling their planned attendance at a concert.

The death of any person is a somber event, and the feelings of those who have lost a close relative are the same the world over. However, the false picture that the news reports presented back in Japan echoed the ones frequently seen during the air strikes on Afghanistan. There were those who turned this tragedy into a simplistic tale of virtue, while others took a critical line as though to say, "See, we told you it was too dangerous." Some Japanese government officials puffed out their chests and spoke of how Japan had made a "noble sacrifice." It was a stupid response.

This incident made me feel perplexed at the way Japan had changed. The

Japan of the good old days was fading away. The notion of respect for human life did not apply to the people of Afghanistan. The spirit of standing with the disadvantaged had gone silent. Times had changed. The opportunistic ways of the new Japan, where people would argue over trivial words and deeds and cast stones, confident in their superior numbers, rubbed me the wrong way. The fact that they made such a performance out of a person's death was the most vexing thing of all. No one could take the place of Itō Kazuya. He was an ordinary young man, but he was also a treasured human being. I wished that people would just let him rest in peace. Those were my true feelings.

However, there was no time for me to indulge in debate. The Marwarid Canal was close to passing through the bedrock at the 20-kilometer point, the most difficult part of the planned course, and the foundations had just been laid for construction of the Sheiwa district mosque and madrassa. Surveys for a long-hoped for intake weir in the Kama district were just about to begin. Above all, it was a critical moment that would determine whether or not tens of thousands of people would return to farming. For me to return to Japan because of the danger was out of the question. PMS had had staff members who were killed or injured before, but it never caused me to halt our work. Too many lives depended on what we were doing.

The talk about pulling out all our Japanese staffers caused a great commotion among them. Up to that point, detailed directions at the work site had been passed on through the Japanese staff. For their part, the Japanese workers had gained self-confidence and a sense of purpose through doing their jobs. They could not imagine how things would go without them. With a tempest of news and rumors swirling around, the uneasiness grew. I was probably the one with the coolest view of the situation. My mind was totally devoted to trying to figure out how to reorganize the work that lay ahead of us. To those who were all riled up, I probably seemed unfeeling.

The difference of views was irreconcilable. It was not a question of which was correct. On the one hand there were the massive numbers of local residents who had no choice but to cling to their homeland and go on living there. On the other hand, there were the foreigners who could distance themselves from the place at any time. That dichotomy could not be changed. Everyone had unhappy thoughts. To feel close to people you know is human nature. Our local team was like a combat unit in these harsh circumstances. It was not reasonable to expect Japanese people to move in lockstep with the locals and demand the same suffering and sacrifices of them. But unless we did, we would not be able to finish our work. My mind went around in circles in trying to find a solution to this dilemma.

At this point, what I felt I had to do was to close the gaps in perception

Local residents attend a memorial service for Itō Kazuya on September 9, 2008.

Assistant Hospital Director Ziaur-Rahman, partners from the agriculture team, and the author offer prayers at a memorial stone for Itō on September 13.

with the Japan side, while simultaneously putting aside all my worries and sentiments and resolutely completing the work on the irrigation canal. I had no alternative. Another urgent matter was to win the release of Itō's driver, who had been arrested on false charges. (He had been abducted together with Itō and then left behind, after which the authorities detained him as a "prime suspect.") His release was obtained after pleading with the provincial governor, but there were still many mysteries, and the truth of what had happened remained shrouded in darkness.

I was absent from Jalalabad for nearly two weeks after the incident, and our staff and workers there became quite despondent. When I returned on September 7 to hastily reorganize the operation, the melancholy atmosphere had spread throughout the staff, and everyone was at their wits' end. The first thing to do was to give each person some concrete task to perform. I turned a blind eye to small failures. The urgent task was to cultivate a team that could faithfully carry out its work.

Meanwhile, however, the parents of our young Japanese workers must have been worried. I decided to move up the schedule for sending them home to September. Also, since I could no longer keep my eye on our base hospital in Peshawar, I resolved to turn it over to the locals there. The security situation there had not become so dire that we had to withdraw completely, but I thought I should not keep the Japanese workers in Afghanistan and Pakistan any longer under the circumstances. Furthermore, having to keep checking to make sure everyone was safe and maintaining lines of communication would interfere with my regular work. It was around this time that two of the operators of our rented heavy machinery were kidnapped and murdered, and more than a few of our local staff and workers were wounded. But the lives of some 100,000 farmers depended on our completing the project. It was our responsibility to make it happen. It would have been unethical to abandon it solely on account of what people were worrying about in Japan.

"Leave vengeance to the Lord. But you reap what you sow." That was my feeling at the time. And sure enough, that is what happened.

Security Conditions in Peshawar Worsen

Meanwhile, the waves of chaos were bearing down quickly even on Peshawar in Pakistan. Starting in spring 2008, substantial numbers of Americans began showing up there; they were clearly involved in some sort of clandestine operation. Twenty thousand rifles were distributed to residents of Bajaur Agency in Pakistan's North-West Frontier Province. This was not covered in any major news reports, but US military sources explained it had been done "so the locals can defend themselves." Around this time, air raids aimed at killing Taliban leaders started being carried out on mosques and madrassas daily. There were frequent hits on mistaken targets, too, which baffled me.

It is easier to start something than to end it, and we are all too often shackled by our past achievements. We had begun considering relocating the PMS Hospital in spring 2007, but for various reasons that effort had come to a standstill. All the work I had put into the facility made me that much more reluctant to let it go. Back in 1998, we had poured all of our energy into building the hospital with the aim of creating a semipermanent base for treating victims of Hansen's disease. Our staff in Japan and in Pakistan, led by Assistant Director Ziaur-Rahman and Acting Director Fujita Chiyoko, devoted themselves with great enthusiasm to the project. We worked hard to train physicians and nurses, while Japanese worker Fujii Takuro put in enormous effort on the administrative side. We eventually created an uncommonly strong organization in the region. At one point, we had twenty-six physicians, twenty assistant nurses, and ten laboratory technicians. We operated clinics in Chitral and Kohistan in Pakistan's North-West Frontier Province, and in Dara-e-Noor, Dara-e-Pech, and Wama (in Nuristan Province) on the Afghan side of the border. After all the foreign aid organizations withdrew from Afghanistan in March 2001, we called the attention of the Taliban administration to the plight of the districts in Kabul that had been left without physicians, and we opened five temporary clinics there. Even amid the US air strikes, we had continued to provide medical care without interruption. The hospital in Peshawar had also been the base for our food distribution program during the air strikes. It was only natural that I had developed an attachment to this familiar haunt.

After the NATO-led International Security Assistance Force (ISAF) began its drive into the provinces of Afghanistan, the security situation deteriorated rapidly. Wherever ISAF forces were encamped, the fighting promptly expanded. In 2005, we closed the Wama clinic in Nuristan and the Dara-e-Pech clinic in Kunar. But our hospital in Peshawar continued to provide support for impoverished residents of eastern Afghanistan, where there was a dearth of decent medical facilities.

Here, too, however, the situation was gradually becoming less secure. By 2007, an insurgency had developed in Swat, which had been the calmest region of the North-West Frontier Province, while anti-government forces had early on made a home base of Waziristan in the southern part of the province. We had been looking into relocating PMS for some time, but due to the confluence of various circumstances and intentions, the move did not progress as anticipated. With the news of Itō's murder, the perception in Japan was that Afghanistan was dangerous, but in truth we were exposed to much greater danger in Peshawar. His death made our withdrawal more urgent, but it was not possible to abruptly wind up our affairs. It was difficult to decide how to deal with our staff, restructure the organization, and handle the enormous amount of administrative work in a short period of time. In the end, the evacuation of the Japanese workers took place in early November 2008, and getting the hospital launched as a separate entity for registration purposes happened in July 2009.

In September 2008, upon hearing that PMS would relocate to Jalalabad in Afghanistan, all one hundred of our staff in Peshawar were devastated. But when a group goes into decline, its last days can be pathetic. The culture in which we were operating considered it a matter of course that in a case like this, unscrupulous people would change their spots and betrayal and plundering would run rampant. I was dumbfounded to see these things occur, but I had to suppress my emotions, still my disquiet, and smoothly push forward with the reorganization effort. I assembled the main clerical and medical staff members and asked for their cooperation. "My friends," I said, "it's been about a decade since we opened this hospital. Many people have been saved thanks to your efforts. Despite the danger to your own lives, you have continued to work bravely and unstintingly, whether in the mountains of Afghanistan or in Kabul amid the air raids. Even after many people left in the wake of the air strikes, those of you who remained have faithfully continued to do your jobs. At this point, the Japanese staff are departing, and we are about to move our headquarters to Jalalabad across the mountains. Now that it has become difficult to cross the border, we cannot know what will happen with our organization under its new structure. However, I cannot forsake you. Those of you who we must unfortunately leave behind here: I ask that you continue as before to devote yourselves to your patients. So far as God permits it, I will be together with all of you."

The person who was busiest to the end was our chief administrative officer, Ikramullah Khan. This serious-minded fifty-five-year-old former army captain was an upright Muslim with a strong sense of duty and humanity. He sympathized deeply with PMS's activities, and enthusiastically gave his unstinting support on an ongoing basis. Amid the chaos of the veritable street-to-street combat in 2009, as those around him fled, he held out on his own and steadily performed his duties. He created our new organization with official provincial approval, and smoothly transferred the setup for dispensing medical care. He had been a military man, so he had an accurate read on the developments in the fighting and passed that on to us.

The PMS Hospital staff.

Acting Director Fujita Chiyoko.

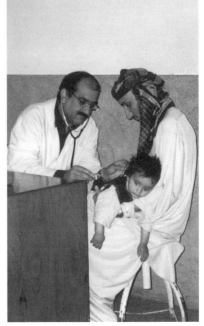

Assistant Director Ziaur-Rahman.

Dr. Ziaur-Rahman, the assistant director, who was forty-eight years old at the time, was to concurrently serve as the PMS office manager. He left his family behind in Peshawar and took up his new post in Jalalabad. He had a fiery temperament and was full of energy. It was he who proposed distributing food during the air strikes and took command of the effort. Jalalabad was his hometown. He made the most of his personal connections in the region and threw himself into the drive to reorganize PMS.

Chapter 8

Setting Our Sights on the Gamberi Desert

The Valley of Death

The Gamberi Desert lies along the border between the provinces of Nangarhar and Laghman in eastern Afghanistan. It covers an area that measures about 4 kilometers across by 20 kilometers long. Situated in the southern foothills of the Keshmand Mountains—a branch of the Hindu Kush range—it has no riverine system with waters that can be counted on to flow in predictable volumes every year. The cumulonimbus clouds of summer can produce unbelievably huge floods two or three times a year. But nature is capricious; in some years they do not come at all.

This desert has been notorious since antiquity as a place where travelers are consigned to oblivion, and thirsty locals will say their throats are "as parched as the Gamberi." Because it offers a shortcut from Jalalabad to Laghman, there have been countless instances of people unfamiliar with the conditions there attempting to walk across it and dying. Looking across the desert from a low hill, you can see villages with greenery spreading on the other side. They seem so close that it is hard to believe they are 20 kilometers away. The farther the incautious traveler goes, the more they will lose their sense of direction and become lost among the sand dunes or in a gully between rocks where they can no longer see what is around them. The intense sunlight beats down on them relentlessly, and before long they become exhausted in this waterless hell and collapse.

The first employee of Peace Japan Medical Services (PMS) to die on the job lost his life because of this desert. Back in 1988, we had a clinician who was from Laghman Province. He had been in Jalalabad, which at the time was a dangerous place because of the fighting that was going on there. He decided he would return to Peshawar by crossing the desert on foot. As he was originally from the area, he was familiar with the local terrain. However, on his way he came across an old man who had collapsed. He picked the man up and carried him on his back. It took a long time for them to cover the dozen-plus kilometers. Just short of the village of Shigi, our colleague died of heat stroke caused by dehydration. The person he was carrying survived. At

The view across the Gamberi Desert, a 4-by-20-kilometer valley of death.

PMS, we regarded our colleague as someone who had died in the line of duty and gave him a funeral with full honors.

In the years that followed, I often passed through this region as I traveled to build our clinics in mountainous regions. Still, the fact that it was the site of our organization's first death on the job left a profound impression on me. This desert did not seem to be anything special at first glance, but because of that incident I always felt there was something eerie about it. Locals feared the area. They believed that demons would whisper things to mislead you, and that ghosts would appear to drive you mad. Even the Soviets in their mighty tanks were said to have feared this place. In fact, near the road the rusted remains of tanks were lying exposed to the sun. The ruts of treads that had spun uselessly were still distinctly visible on the sand dunes. One could only imagine what had happened to the crew. That made it all the more eerie.

When we opened the 13-kilometer-long phase-one section of the Marwarid Canal in April 2007, one of the senior workers, Ghulam Sakhi (nicknamed Tarafdar), had asked me, "How much farther will we go?" Given that we had yet to finish our studies and surveys for phase two of the project, I answered, "As far as we can." Tarafdar, who had formerly been a teacher at a military school, was an incorruptible Pashtun with the tenacity of a bulldog and a hatred of wrongdoing. He was a stalwart figure who coolly executed his duties even during the fury of bombings. Now, pointing far off in the distance, he smiled and said, "You can't mean that we'll go to the Gamberi Desert, can you?"

"Actually," I said, "we might go there. However far we go, it will be as God guides us."

At this, he burst into laughter.

"Okay, Doctor Sahib, let's go! I am at your disposal to the very end. Gamberi, or Japan, or to the ends of the earth. This time, instead of bombs we have ghosts to deal with."

In short, he thought I was joking.

In April 2007, when we celebrated the completion of phase one, I told the team, which included the Japanese workers Honda Jun'ichirō and Shindō Yōichirō, to proceed with surveying the course for phase two. When they hit the 19-kilometer point in June, I received surprising news. On June 10, the survey team—which had already reached bedrock at the mouth of the Gamberi Desert—reported that we could irrigate a vast expanse of that barren land by simply running the canal aboveground for another 2 kilometers at a height of a dozen meters or so.

At the time, we had no access to such tools as a global-positioning system or satellite maps. The team relied solely on leveling tools as they proceeded, inchworm-like, to determine the planned slopes as well as the positions and height differences for siphons. Initially, judging by visual inspection, I thought reaching the Gamberi Desert was impossible. I believed the most we could do was provide water for the natural floodway at the entrance to the desert.

Thinking perhaps a survey error had led to the conclusion that the desert could be watered, I ordered that the survey be reconfirmed. On June 12, together with Honda and Shindō, I went to check the 19-kilometer point where the survey ended. When I asked, "Where is the planned level spot for the bed of the canal?" they showed me a survey point marked on a small hill. I cannot forget how amazed I was—I felt as though I was staring across the boundless surface of the moon. The planned line of the irrigation canal was to pass approximately 18 meters above the base of the bedrock hill. From atop that steep, rocky prominence, what lay before me was a veritable ocean of sand with the horizon stretching across in the far-off distance. Aside from a few small hills, the landscape was all sand dunes. The temperature that day was 52° C, and the combination of the hot winds blowing and the sunlight reflecting off the white sand made my eyes hurt. Could this possibly be turned into a green space? If that were possible, I would put my trust in God wholeheartedly. Our Afghan staff hugged one another, overjoyed. "*Allahu akbar!*" they cried out. "God is great!"

Thus, it was decided that the route for going into the desert would be located 7 kilometers from the end point of the phase-one construction and 19 kilometers from the intake gate at the starting point of the canal. In short, we had realized that if we could go into the desert for about 4.8 kilometers—getting past a 2-kilometer stretch of bedrock and then traversing the desert for another 2.8 kilometers—the resulting canal would easily open 1,000 hectares of land to cultivation. Tarafdar was surprised, but this new prospect stirred him into action. "I'm more than sixty years old and I have nothing else to wish for—I just want to see the water flowing before I die," he said, throwing himself totally into the effort.

For locals, the thought of irrigating the Gamberi Desert seemed almost like a miracle. Before we knew it, "To Gamberi!" had become the watchword among the staff. As the political situation around us gradually worsened, this project remained a sole ray of hope. The PMS staff and local residents joined forces and worked for all they were worth.

Organizing the Construction

I was still under pressure to wrap up the first phase of our construction project—specifically, the work on the intake weirs and embankments along the river. But

Route of the Marwarid Canal

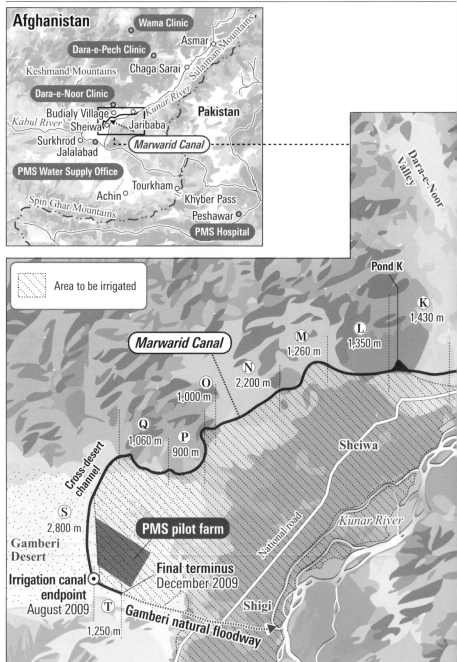

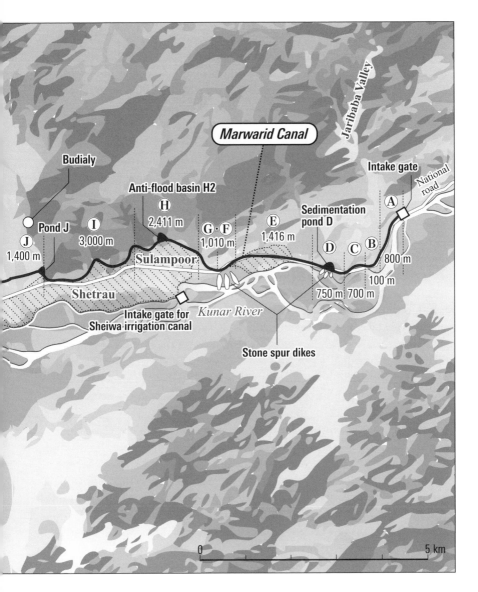

by this time our teams had almost perfected their canal-building skills. Excavating, filling, lining (i.e., preparing the bed of the irrigation canal), preparing and installing gabions, creating live-willow revetments—whatever the task was, all we had to do was give the responsible team the relevant diagrams, and the work would be carried out almost entirely to satisfaction. We had also established methods and standards for building water gates, siphons, and other such concrete structures, and our workers had developed into a skilled cohort.

We usually had four hundred workers available, and at times we could count on more than five hundred. We split them up into teams of about twenty to thirty, with a regular office staffer present to oversee their work. A survey team was on site to take the lead in meticulously determining levels and guiding the excavators, who would get the bedrock chipped away with jackhammers. If the ground was already fairly even, they would dig roughly or fill as necessary. The next team would then reconfirm that the ground was level and then line the canal bed and work on the embankments and the roads running alongside them. A third team would prepare gabion baskets for use along the sides of the waterway, decide where they should be placed, and pack them with stone. Finally, a fourth team would create the live-willow revetments around the area where the water was to come in. This efficient division of labor came about more or less naturally. With regard to the concrete structures, our Japanese workers Suzuki Manabu and Kondō Shin'ichi trained a team well enough that they could handle their work satisfactorily to match the plan they were given.

As to mechanical equipment, I cannot say that we were happy with what we had. Still, whenever some piece of equipment broke down, the workers would simply take up pickaxes and shovels. If a cement mixer stopped working, a human wave of workers would assemble to do the mixing. If a shovel broke, then they would go to work on the earth and stone with their bare hands. The dramatic improvements to working efficiency we achieved came about not due solely to mechanical power but also thanks to the determination of our workers.

Furthermore, transporting earth and stone required the use of material resources like fuel. We kept an eye on how each team was proceeding with its work so that we could deliver the right amounts of red soil, stone for the gabions, and gravel for the concrete at the appropriate time to make the work go smoothly. The bulk of the material resources went toward tasks around the river, the greatest part expended on transporting boulders. I assigned a team of five staff members to oversee delivery from the quarrying site to the destination. I oversaw the river works directly myself and appointed my driver Mokhtar to be my aide; he was in charge when I was absent. We needed

Work on the irrigation canal was done methodically and efficiently through division of labor.

enormous numbers of boulders, and so much was uncertain about the task that they were accounting for much of our budget. I was forced to make decisions by thinking about a budget measured in hundreds of millions of yen while trying not to waste money or materials. I was also the one to decide the suitable point at which to wind up particular jobs. Half the budget went toward heavy machinery, and around 80 percent of the stone deliveries were for work around the river.

The chain of command we developed for the construction site is presented in the accompanying chart (created in August 2008). With this in place, phase two of construction moved ahead with unstoppable force. It took a little more than a year to complete the 4-plus kilometers of work—starting in April 2007 and ending in July 2008—that brought us to the edge of the Gamberi Desert.

By no means did we work like this from the outset. It took some trial and error before we were organized in a way that achieved a natural equilibrium. Our Japanese workers joined up with the various sections and helped in their efforts. Aside from the irrigation canal and river works, we also had our pilot farm and the Dara-e-Noor clinic. Our staff veteran Takahashi Osamu oversaw the farm, while Assistant Director Ziaur-Rahman handled the clinic.

The parts of the irrigation canal that had already been completed were subject to frequent floods and flash floods, and so they required maintenance. However, these events also proved the canal's durability, and that in turn gave our staff and workers greater confidence. We also gradually refined our construction methods. When we combined the use of gabion walls for the irrigation canal with willow revetments, the canal could easily hold up against ordinary flash floods. The concrete structures were made to withstand flooding, and not one of them suffered damage. The workers became masters at handling repairs, and it seemed that reaching the Gamberi Desert was simply a matter of funds and time. Back in Japan, the Peshawar-kai was fully with us on this project, and they continued their ardent efforts to publicize what we were doing and solicit donations.

Then, in August 2008, Itō was abducted and killed. As I explained in the previous chapter, our local workers became despondent about our subsequent sudden decision to pull out our Japanese staff, and this brought the organization to the verge of falling apart. If our group lost its purpose, its willpower, and its management structure, no matter how technically proficient our workers now were, they would fall into disarray. I was fighting delicate battles on two fronts as I worked to hand over the PMS Hospital in Peshawar while simultaneously totally reorganizing the irrigation canal construction effort. However, our dedication and the work of so many people helping us in Afghanistan made it possible to do both.

Construction Site Chain of Command and Construction Details

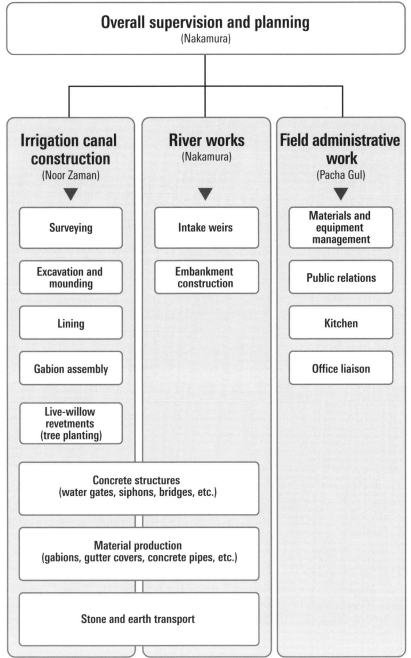

Overall supervision and planning
(Nakamura)

Irrigation canal construction
(Noor Zaman)

- Surveying
- Excavation and mounding
- Lining
- Gabion assembly
- Live-willow revetments (tree planting)

River works
(Nakamura)

- Intake weirs
- Embankment construction

Field administrative work
(Pacha Gul)

- Materials and equipment management
- Public relations
- Kitchen
- Office liaison

Concrete structures
(water gates, siphons, bridges, etc.)

Material production
(gabions, gutter covers, concrete pipes, etc.)

Stone and earth transport

"If You Are Virtuous, You Will Not Be Lonely":
The Spirit of Our Partners

The Marwarid Canal succeeded thanks to the extraordinary cooperation we received from local people. Without the efforts of those who chose to remain in the background, the project undoubtedly would have come to a standstill. Just when I least expected it, the good faith that so often remains hidden would suddenly emerge. These people strongly believed in helping PMS. They supported our project, acting in the face of dangerous conditions without a thought to making a profit.

Our biggest expenditures were for heavy machinery and dump trucks, which accounted for more than half of the construction costs. This was another of our budgetary concerns. However, in these matters, too, PMS was blessed with good luck. The main people standing in the shadows here were the equipment operators and the managers of the companies that rented us heavy machinery. At a work site where mechanical power was scarce, much depended on the technical skills of the excavator and loader operators. In particular, excavator operations determined not only how efficiently our work would get done, but also whether or not our intake weirs and embankments would function as planned. How the boulders transported to the site were placed, oriented, and packed together depended entirely on the skills of the operators.

In not a few cases, rental company owners were reluctant to have their equipment used to transport boulders, or would decline to be involved in the river work. They were worried about how easily their equipment could be damaged and the amount of gasoline they would need. In this context, we were much obliged to one outstanding individual, Haji Bismillah, the president of a heavy-machinery company. Small of stature and with a kindly smile, he was a person of influence in Paktia Province due to his standing as a devout Muslim and a wise elder around fifty years of age. Immediately after the collapse of the Taliban regime, he recognized that construction work would provide an enormous source of revenue, and so he launched his heavy machinery rental business. His clan were major landholders in the region, but the water shortage, which was also affecting Paktia, was making it impossible for their tenant farmers to sustain themselves.

There was a period shortly after we began the canal construction project when a road-building project was proceeding right next to our construction site. Anti-government forces were very much opposed to that project, and the engineers and contractor companies working on it were attacked quite frequently. Even two of the heavy machinery operators working on our project

The construction crew built sturdy embankments for the canal using a combination of gabion walls and live-willow revetments.

The concrete structures were made to withstand flooding and flash floods.

were abducted—one in 2006 and another in 2009—and later found dead. These incidents were due to misunderstandings by the guilty parties.

When one faction of armed insurgents attacked Bismillah's parents' home in Paktia in 2009, he did not waver a bit. He counterattacked, heading a militia of several thousand villagers, and forced the insurgents to agree to leave the PMS construction project alone. He wholeheartedly threw his entire company behind our undertaking after this. There were no indications that he was profiting unduly—to the contrary, I believe he was in the red. He would hold a party for PMS staff and workers every time the canal reached an important milestone, and he shared in our joys and sorrows. He told me, "Doctor, use the heavy machinery however you want to. My operators are your soldiers, so employ them as you wish." We always had more than sixty of his machinery operators and maintenance personnel with us. They lived in flimsy tents through both blistering heat and bitter cold, and they were sincere in their efforts on our behalf. The machinery operators also became noticeably more proficient as the work progressed, and they reached the point where they could understand the purpose behind my designs. In particular, the work around the rivers had no margin for error. I learned how to operate an excavator so I could show them what I wanted done; by following my example they were able to do the work as desired. And loafing on the job gradually became a thing of the past.

Local Government Support

As for our relations with local authorities, the Irrigation Department for Nangarhar Province was a powerful supporter, and they helped us in more ways than one. In 2007, when we finished phase one of the canal project, PMS had a poor reputation among local civil servants. You see, we were not paying the bribes that heartless bureaucrats had come to expect. Afghanistan is a hierarchical society. The general population and their political leaders usually live in different worlds. Even if we had popular support, that did not mean that the government administrators who hailed from the upper classes would necessarily feel warm toward us. To the contrary, from the start they tended to regard us Japanese as "easy touches." They took advantage of their authority to make one unreasonable demand after the other.

To be fair, I should note that foreign organizations in Afghanistan often had their eyes focused on their home countries, and their involvement tended to be fleeting. Afghan government officials knew this as well, and they treated them accordingly. This made it appear to parties both domestic and foreign that the situation in Afghanistan revolved solely around the use of money.

However, within the government there were also many conscientious officials who were disgusted with the rampant corruption and would stand up for us whenever possible. For example, when Delawal Khan was appointed director of the Nangarhar Province Irrigation Department in 2006, he frequently dispatched his confidant, an engineer named Khalid, to check in on us. Khalid had previously been involved with our canal project for two years as a site supervisor. Later, Khan would visit on his own and offer encouragement. (Such visits were rare in Afghanistan; most senior officials feared the possibility of assassination and would not come out into the field.) Khan, a Pashtun from Jalalabad, came from a distinguished family named Sayaf. Around fifty-five years old, he had a well-tended beard and the character and dignity of an elder. He was a devout Muslim like Bismillah, and likewise hated dishonesty. He stood out in a world where doing business through bribes for this and that was a fact of life. Thanks to his presence, any false charges against PMS would be withdrawn at the provincial government level, and never turned into a major controversy.

Still, some senior officials were uncomfortable with Khan's presence, and he frequently experienced various hardships because of this. His son was even trapped and arrested on suspicion of being involved with anti-government forces. However, the provincial governor feared assassination. He recognized that so long as he had this man who was respected locally in his inner circle he would be safe, and so he kept Khan close at hand. Khan was our sympathizer within the government until 2012, when he decided to resign of his own accord. He then volunteered his services as an advisor to our organization, and in that capacity he kept a sharp eye on local government officials for us. From then on, PMS's influence spread within the local government. And when we began our joint project with the Japan International Cooperation Agency (JICA), organs of the government in Kabul that had all been antagonistic to us—the Agriculture Ministry, the Irrigation Department, and the Ministry of Finance (responsible for foreign NGOs)—changed course and became our allies. They did this because the engineers who were dispatched on survey missions reported the real situation to them.

Our Local Staff

Assistant Director Ziaur-Rahman actively engaged in liaising with the authorities. The battles behind the scenes in a world so amazingly filled with intrigues might make for interesting talk, but actually dealing with the scheming was extremely exhausting. In fact, "countering intrigues" would be a more accurate description of his work than "liaison." It was beyond the ken of non-Afghans. This is a country where deliberate mutual interference is a common practice; I have encountered it constantly over the past thirty years. The bigger our projects grew, the greater and more systematic the intrigues became. We came to have more friends, and more enemies as well.

Dr. Ziaur-Rahman had shared his fate with ours for two decades. He was loyal to PMS. He was not only conscientiously sympathetic to our aims, but he also skillfully went about winning us supporters and smoothly took care of administrative matters for us. Particularly after we moved to his hometown of Jalalabad, he did not hesitate to make enemies in his efforts to swiftly and skillfully solve problems and manage our business affairs with acumen. He swept aside any systemic antagonisms toward us, and effectively shielded us. His skill at dealing with political matters was a major reason for our ability to make steady progress on our construction project even as the security situation deteriorated.

Dr. Ziaur-Rahman's right-hand man was a former teacher named Pacha Gul; he handled the liaising work on site. A member of the Shinwari tribe hailing from the Achin district, he had been an official with the border guard in Tourkham during the years of the Taliban regime. He was friendly toward us and helped us in various ways in that role. When the Taliban government fell, he lost his job and, hard pressed, he sought one with us at PMS. He was steadfastly honest, quick to seize any opportunities that presented themselves, and mature in character. A skilled negotiator, he involved himself in just about every dispute that came up with locals in the course of our canal project, making it possible for us to keep moving forward. After the Gamberi Desert had been opened, he then took on an important role in looking after conditions in the marshlands. His skillful work on resolving conflicts made him a key player in restoring 500 hectares of farmland.

When we worked on opening the Gamberi, we employed Soorat Mir— the younger brother of the leader of a powerful Laghman Province strongman named Hazrat Ali—as our security guard. Working together with Pacha Gul, he brought order to this otherwise lawless newly opened area. His presence was particularly indispensable when it came to sorting out the rotation for access to irrigation water and guaranteeing that certain areas (forested areas and roads) would be set aside for community use. Unlike his brother, Soorat Mir was a farmer by nature, and he was among the first to move to the Gamberi Desert. He had been eking out an existence there using just well water, so when the Marwarid Canal opened he was overjoyed and happy to give us a hand. He invited his relatives to move nearby and expand the village. Thanks

Delawal Khan, former director of the Nangarhar Province Irrigation Department. (Second from right.)

Assistant Director Ziaur-Rahman (left) and Chief Administrative Officer Ikramullah Khan (center).

to his presence, violent armed groups stayed away from the Gamberi Desert, and the area developed into a pillar of stability under the PMS umbrella.

In Pakistan, we had Ikramullah Khan. He was the chief administrator for the former PMS Hospital in Peshawar, and he kept us informed of trends in that area. He was another devout Muslim who had a favorable impression of us from his time working at the hospital. Even after our move to Jalalabad, he remained consistently solicitous toward us. Knowing that construction projects that affect rivers and water use can lead to conflict between nations, he worked hard from the Pakistani side to help ensure that no serious difficulties would arise. For a while there were groundless rumors that anyone who got involved with these water-related projects would be assassinated by an intelligence service, which understandably made the staff uneasy. Ikram helped dispel this anxiety. As a former army man, he remained friends with various active-duty senior officers, and he spared no effort to provide us advice on various matters.

Finally, the embassies of Afghanistan and Pakistan in Japan were also well disposed toward us. One senior official who would go from being Afghanistan's health minister to his country's ambassador to Japan had once been a patient of mine, and he was unstinting with his support, both publicly and privately.

"You Are the Ones Who Are Dangerous"

On top of that, I should note that there were even some US military officers who were friendly toward us. For example, in March 2009 the US Army's Provincial Reconstruction Team (PRT) communicated to us through the provincial Agriculture Department a plan to create a fish farm in one of the irrigation canal's sedimentation ponds. If such a thing were created, it would no longer be possible to adjust the amount of water flowing in the canal, spoiling the canal's utility and creating problems for the farmers living in the watershed. The notification, which had an overbearing and peremptory tone, came just after newly elected US President Barack Obama had declared that he would shift the priority in the "War on Terror" from Iraq to Afghanistan, and the number of soldiers in the ISAF had just been increased to reach 120,000. The PRT was being quite high-handed. If the matter was handled poorly, the hard-pressed farmers would not stand by in silence. Still, my absolute policy was to avoid violence, and so we reluctantly used gabions to make a high wall around the mouth of the sedimentation pond that mutely declared entry was forbidden. We then pulled together a fifty-person-strong team to start planting a massive number of trees around the pond.

In the nick of time, with our project under threat, perhaps because of a report from the provincial Agriculture Department, the PRT gave some ground and said they wanted to hear an explanation from me. Having been summoned to their office in Jalalabad, I strove to provide one.

I told the PRT, "The irrigation canal provides the foundations for the livelihoods of tens of thousands of farmers. There are many other, much better places elsewhere for fish farms. But if you want to take it by force, then take it. No one can stand up to the strongest army in the world. We will wash our hands of the matter and get out. However, you will have to take full responsibility for how the people who live along canal react. What's more, it is not a safe place."

"You mean the Taliban show up there?"

"No, foreign armies launch attacks."

"You mean us?"

"Yes."

"We only patrol to maintain security."

"That's not the case. You were the ones who machine-gunned us there."

There was a commotion among the officers. One officer in his mid-thirties looked at me with an expression that seemed to say, "Oh, you're still around, too?" and spoke up.

"That's true," he said. "I was here five years ago, in November 2003. If that's when you're talking about, I remember the incident well. The army promised to establish areas restricting air traffic to prevent a recurrence of such accidents, but it didn't happen. There were also repeated instances of armored cars tumbling into the river near the storage reservoir there." In the end, the fish-farm proposal was retracted and was never put into effect.

Two years later, in response to an invitation from a UN-related organization, I attended a conference where I had the chance to rub elbows with that officer again. Bored at the tediously long-winded discussion, I happened to cast a glance sideways and there he was, also trying to suppress a yawn.

"They want to talk about how to improve social services at this point? . . . It's too late. Those of us who missed our chance to get out of Afghanistan have been left holding the bag," he whispered to me with a wink. After the conference, I was surrounded by uniformed junior PRT officers who offered friendly looks as they reached out to shake my hand. This was just before the PRT's office in Jalalabad was closed. They no longer wanted to be involved with what was anything but a "reconstruction" effort by the army. But they seemed to be happy about the expanding stretch of greenery alongside the irrigation canal, which could now be seen from the air.

The organizers of the conference were proposing weekly meetings. I responded, "This is hardly the time for that sort of thing. Given how fluid the situation is, what would we gather to talk about? Both those providing help and those being helped are completely exhausted. Even once every few months might be too much." This also seemed to resonate deeply with the PRT officers. They knew full well about the realities in Afghanistan, but they did not have the freedom to dismiss the proposal as empty talk.

Though our positions were very different, I encountered a good number of people with sound judgment even among foreign military personnel like these officers. Everyone was already fed up with this unproductive conflict. The people who were making a fuss were the faraway politicians and critics who knew nothing of conditions on the front lines.

There is much about the tremendous efforts being made behind the scenes that I cannot make public. If I were to do so, idle commentators back in Japan would simply pick up on isolated words and argue about them, and that would invite misunderstanding. The reality cannot be explained by logic alone, but Japanese commentators tend to look at matters only from a theoretical perspective. That is why I cannot put my trust in them. In any event, it is precisely because of such behind-the-scenes efforts that PMS has received support from a broad network of people in Afghanistan ranging from farmers to government ministers, and transcending such political frameworks as "pro-government" or "anti-government." It is no exaggeration to say that our work was a product of support that went beyond the boundaries of nation, race, and social status. Some may see our approach as unprincipled pandering to all comers. They are free to think so if they wish. But I see it as evidence of something precious that is common to all human beings. Equality and rights are perfectly legitimate values to uphold. But our ethics as human beings, which I believe to be universal, come before those values. These ethics are informed by something sacred—something that transcends simple arguments about good and evil.

The Miracle Reaches the Desert
2009 AND BEYOND

Chapter 9

The Blessings of the Earth—Opening the Canal

Creating Reservoirs

I will now bring this story back to the Gamberi Desert.

In October 2008, we passed the 19-kilometer mark on the Marwarid Canal and started on the most difficult part of the dig. This was a roughly 2-kilometer-long segment consisting of zone P, measuring 900 meters, and zone Q, measuring 1,060 meters. The canal would snake along the side of a soaring outcropping of bedrock at an average elevation of 14 meters from ground level on its way to the edge of the desert. The terrain here was similar to what we had found in the FG segment at the 4.8-kilometer point where we entered the Sulampoor Plain in 2005. However, this was on a grander scale.

Scale was not the only problem; there was something more difficult here. Certainly, the 1-kilometer-long FG segment was a difficult spot. With a height of 17 meters and a base that measured 50 meters across, the canal at that point required an enormous amount of filling work on its base. But the bedrock outcropping was not particularly high, so we did not have to worry about the effects of rainfall pouring down the side of the outcropping into the waterway. Here in the PQ segment, though, we were working amid rugged mountains towering 800 meters, and there were numerous valleys through which flash floods would flow. Three of these valleys were particularly deep and wide. If any concentrated downpour occurred, the result would be a flash flood of unbelievable volume pouring into the desert.

One must bear in mind that a desert is not simply an uninhabitable place that lacks water. The localized cloudbursts that struck this area capriciously in summer would quickly wash away anything in their path. The area on which rain typically fell in this region was fairly small, and so the total amount of rainfall was not that great, but it would be channeled into stony valleys with steep slopes of 45 degrees or more and no water retention capability. The raging currents would break through the canal in one stroke, and the floodwaters would surge toward the human settlements below. Accordingly, we worked from maps to estimate the size of the rainfall area and the volumes of water that each valley could anticipate, and decided to implement a two-pronged strategy of planting trees to mitigate flows and collecting the water in large reservoirs before feeding it into the canal. If just deflecting flash floods had been the aim, then we could have run the water through siphons, but we wanted to both irrigate and to mitigate flood damage in these bedrock surroundings, so we took a new approach in designing the canal.

We created reservoirs named P, Q2, and Q3 at three locations in the largest of the valleys. The largest of these was Q2. Measuring 360 meters long and 180 meters across, and with embankments that stood 17 meters high, it blocked the valley. This largest reservoir was a type of fill dam. It was based on old reservoirs I had seen around Japan; I thought something similar would work for us in Afghanistan. Its surface area when full would be around 30,000 square meters. Even if there was a concentrated downpour of, say, 50 millimeters per hour, inferring from the size of the rainfall area we estimated that the water in the reservoir would rise by no more than 20 to 30 centimeters.

In Japan, the mountains are covered with abundant forests and the soil retains a certain proportion of the water from a rainfall. Furthermore, the rainwater travels down through innumerable stands of trees, and this reduces its speed as it flows down into valleys. Thus, the very land of Japan itself protects human settlements thanks to the water retention capability of its forests. Furthermore, the trees have fostered the accumulation of rich soil with the tremendous amounts of mulch that they produce.

In Afghanistan, the conditions we faced were quite the opposite. The rocky mountainsides have little vegetation, and flash floods rush down them with furious velocity. We adopted the following strategies to cope with this:

(1) Make the surface of each reservoir as broad as possible to increase the volume of water that can be stored.
(2) Afforest the reservoir's surroundings to reduce the speed of rainwater flowing in.
(3) Increase the velocity of the canal current in the area of dangerous bedrock to quickly discharge water from the reservoir.
(4) To cope with the unlikely event of an inundation, create flood-control basins directly below the backslope side of the embankments, and set up a broad riverine buffer strip.

In short, our strategy was one of flood mitigation.

Once we actually began the work, however, we found we would need an enormous quantity of materials. We estimated that we would require 280,000 cubic meters of earth and stone for the levee at Q2 alone. Mohammad Naeem, the veteran staffer who was supervising Q2, thought at first that I was joking. He was at a loss for words when I put him in charge of the reservoir.

"This is a major project just by itself, isn't it?" he asked.

"Let's allow another year for it," I replied. "We took around two years to do the area by the bedrock in sections F and G."

Naheem had started out as a guard for our living quarters, but we valued his ability to read and write and so switched him over to managing the work site. He had an affable and tenacious disposition, and never fought with anyone. He was ideally suited for the protracted embankment work on the canal, and he carried out the job that he said he would for however many years were necessary. He had a moon face and thick eyebrows, which prompted the Japanese workers to nickname him Saigō Takamori for his resemblance to the Japanese general who rose to prominence near the end of the Tokugawa shogunate. He was poor and had a family to support, so he had been discouraged about becoming unemployed when the Japanese staff pulled out. However, being assigned this major responsibility restored him to high spirits.

Seepage was another issue. Unlike at our previous reservoirs, here there were steep slopes where coarse-grained sandy soil would settle out and pile up at the base of the bedrock. Water would naturally leak through this sandy layer. While "leakage" may not sound good, at both rivers and artificial water-use facilities like canals and reservoirs, some of the water permeates the ground underneath. This seepage becomes a source of the groundwater that flows invisibly underground. In the case of irrigation canals, the water lost due to this is reckoned as "seepage loss"; it normally amounts to 30 percent of the flow. This is why, when the canal was opened, we saw an increase in the groundwater of the surrounding area, the level of water in the wells rose, and the surrounding trees grew more readily.

The amount of seepage depends on topographical conditions. In places with coarse sand and gravel, the water seeps in more readily; if the grains are finer, like those found in red soil, then the water does not seep in so well. At places where the irrigation canal runs close to a river, the amount of water in the canal might also increase due to seepage from the river. Normally, it is not possible to see seepage water or groundwater flowing, but depending on the terrain, the water can spout forth from the surface of the earth to produce fountains and springs.

Seepage occurs at reservoirs as well. Large amounts of water will pour through a poorly constructed levee like a sieve, causing it to weaken and eventually burst. At reservoir Q2, the levee was to be sitting directly above a place where the ground consisted of several meters of coarse sandy soil. Moreover, the water level in the reservoir would rise to a dozen or so meters above the

Marwarid Canal Terminus

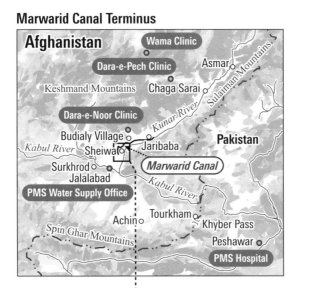

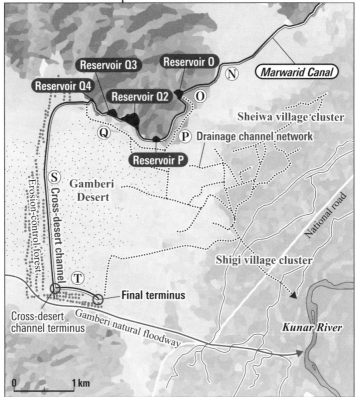

ground. If the reservoir were ever neglected, seepage water under high pressure would work its way through the bottom of the levee and eventually create a hole through which massive amounts of reservoir water would spout forth.

To prevent this from happening, we replaced the sandy soil with a clay-rich layer down to a level that would be difficult for the water to permeate. Doing this would dramatically reduce the amount of seepage. However, the levee itself could not consist only of red soil. As the seepage line rose, the clay would absorb greater amounts of water and turn mushy, and eventually the levee would breach. In Japan, this phenomenon is regarded as a major cause of breaches in embankments along rivers following heavy rains.

Accordingly, we basically applied the following three principles:

(1) Spread a low-permeability layer of clay-rich red soil on the inner slope of the levee to reduce the volume of percolating water (i.e., blanket work).
(2) To ensure that the core of the levee is not only impermeable but also strong, create a hard material for it by mixing stones in with the red soil.
(3) Cover the outer slope with a thick, broad layer of gravel so any water that does seep into the levee will promptly flow out (i.e., drainage work).

In short, the inner slope, facing the reservoir, should be made difficult to permeate, while the outer slope should allow any water that has seeped into the levee to be swiftly discharged. These principles probably have gone unchanged since time immemorial.

Be that as it may, the amounts in question here were anything but ordinary. We would exhaust ourselves, fervently doing the filling work as we poured in the water and watched the amount of seepage, repeatedly reinforcing the levee further. Our patient efforts to do the work around the bedrock—with Q2 in particular being critical for us—had begun. The width of the lower part of this levee would measure around 100 meters. It would rise with gently sloped sides; the levee crown would be about 15 meters wide, while the levee as a whole would stand about 17 meters tall and run for a length of 360 meters. It was the largest of the embankments that we handled.

Embarking on a construction project of this scale was nerve-racking, and of course I was worried about our ability to pull it off. Happily, there were many old reservoirs of this type near my home back in Ōmuta in Fukuoka. I traveled around looking at them once more to be certain. One of these old

Creating a Reservoir Levee to Last

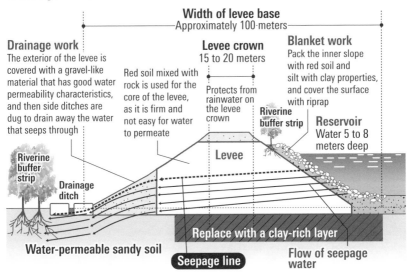

Width of levee base
—Approximately 100-meters—

Drainage work
The exterior of the levee is covered with a gravel-like material that has good water permeability characteristics, and then side ditches are dug to drain away the water that seeps through

Red soil mixed with rock is used for the core of the levee, as it is firm and not easy for water to permeate

Levee crown
15 to 20 meters

Protects from rainwater on the levee crown

Blanket work
Pack the inner slope with red soil and silt with clay properties, and cover the surface with riprap

Riverine buffer strip

Reservoir
Water 5 to 8 meters deep

Riverine buffer strip

Drainage ditch

Levee

Replace with a clay-rich layer

Water-permeable sandy soil

Seepage line

Flow of seepage water

Blanket work underway at reservoir Q2.

reservoirs had the peculiar name of Rokunin-zutsumi (six-person reservoir). It is said that until recently it was a place where people would go to commit suicide. Many Christians apparently lived in this area—part of the Miike domain—in the early modern period. It is directly across from the Shimabara Peninsula, which was home to a major concentration of Christian converts. After their faith was banned early in the seventeenth century, the Christians of the peninsula staged the unsuccessful Shimabara Rebellion, which was followed by intensified persecution in Miike as well. According to local history, around that time there was a Christian family whose daughter was being sought after by a local magistrate even though she was already betrothed. The six members of the family chose to throw themselves into the reservoir rather than submit to the magistrate's will, thus giving rise to the reservoir's name. The reservoir therefore already existed in the early seventeenth century; its longevity suggests how much effort went into building it.

People in those days probably relied solely on experience in constructing such reservoirs. These simple structures generally measured from 100 to 150 meters in length, and the levees were made of red soil and gravel. The examples that remain today have probably been repaired countless times, but the key element was vegetation. There were always thick woods in the vicinity, and stands of pussy willows or Japanese nutmeg would grow naturally on the inner slopes. The bottoms of reservoirs that have run dry show evidence that gravel and mud sedimented and gradually stabilized them. Stones and rocks were used to create the framework, and then a layer of clay was packed into the cracks. Also, in many cases stone walls would be created on the outer slope of the levee and would continue on into terraced rice paddies. Almost certainly, the seepage from the reservoir was meant to flow into those paddies.

I was convinced we could do it if we took the time. Construction proceeded as we prepared the drainage channels for seepage water. After repeated ups and downs, we were able to tentatively fill the reservoirs with water in May 2009. However, we had to conduct repairs on them five times, and did not consider the project done until a year and a half later in February 2010. I estimate that around twenty thousand dump-truck loads of fill were required. We poured unimaginable quantities of material resources into the work, and planted many, many trees around the reservoirs—about fifteen thousand for Q2 alone. A number of times the area was hit with concentrated downpours, and we were terrified that one of the reservoirs would fail. They held up, however, and they have now become beautiful lakes surrounded by trees. The experience we acquired through this part of the project would later be put to use in building embankments and dealing with seepage water elsewhere. It was a big help.

An Erosion-Control Forest

Around the time we were struggling with the construction in the areas around the bedrock, work had also begun in parallel on the project to dig a 2.8-kilometer cross-desert channel (section S). Our project to create an erosion-control forest along the channel was also moving forward. On November 9, 2008, we had held a tree-planting ceremony.

It is said that the village of Shigi, which is adjacent to the Gamberi Desert, used to be uninhabitable owing to the searing winds and sandstorms that blew in from that barren waste. Some forty years ago, when the country was on the brink of civil war, the Daoud regime had started planting tamarisk trees, which are resistant to dry conditions, to create a 5-kilometer-long riverine buffer strip. At a width of 300 to 500 meters, the new forest separated Shigi from the Gamberi, protecting the settlement. The tree-planting project was continued by successive regimes before the Taliban finally halted it.

Our channel was located in the desert about 3 or 4 kilometers from the buffer strip. It appeared to us that any desert reclamation project would be impossible without creating an erosion-control forest of a similar scale. Accordingly, we began planting trees at the far side of the area we hoped to reclaim. It would become the front line of the reclamation project. Initially, we relied on tanker trucks to water the trees, but they were costly and did not provide enough water. So, when work on the channel brought it closer, we created a small branch waterway especially for the forest. The trees grew rapidly. As of this writing in May 2013, the buffer strip is several hundred meters wide and 5 kilometers long, and has trees that have grown 10 meters tall. In total, we planted more than 750,000 trees along the 25-kilometer length of the canal. Around 200,000 of those are the tamarisks that make up the Gamberi erosion-control forest.

Tamarisks are wondrous trees. They grow well in desert areas, and can achieve heights of 10 meters or more in the space of four or five years. Their wood is hard, and can be used as fuel. But if planted at the water's edge, they just grow into shrubs standing 1–2 meters tall. In early summer, they sprout clusters of tiny red flowers. They grow in a quest for moist soil underground, and they stop growing once they reach the groundwater layer.

Accordingly, "willows for along the water, tamarisks for the desert" gradually became our standard procedure. In the Old Testament, it is written that the prophet Abraham planted tamarisks. The tree would seem to have quite a long history in the Middle East. Closer to water, we planted eucalyptus trees along with willows. Eucalyptuses became a problem, however, and we limited them to

Water enters reservoir Q2. (May 2009.)

Reservoir Q2 surrounded by woods. (May 2013.)

The author, accompanied by the team members responsible for the tree planting, atop Peace Hill looking down on the Gamberi Desert.

Erosion-control forests of tamarisk planted in the Gamberi Desert, three years after planting was begun.

places where we needed fast results. The issue in our experience was that when eucalyptuses flourish excessively, they block sunlight and hinder the growth of other kinds of vegetation. Furthermore, since their roots are shallow, they topple easily in sudden gusts of wind. Later, following the idea of indigenous vegetation advanced by botanist Miyawaki Akira, we found trees that are considered native to the area, such as *biera* (a low tree that grows naturally in the desert) and *shisham* (sissoo) and began to cultivate seedlings in large quantities. Our plan is to plant them in place of eucalyptuses over an extended period of time.

Opening the Irrigation Canal

Work on the canal made steady progress amid turbulent conditions. We had planned to open the entire canal by spring 2009, but due to the various circumstances I have already mentioned, the completion date was pushed back again and again. Our initial plan was to end the canal after reaching the far side of the Gamberi Desert at a point 23.6 kilometers from the inlet gate. At that point the water would pour into a natural floodway leading back to the Kunar River.

I had wanted to finish in the spring because I thought it would be impossible to work in the hot sands of the desert during the summer. So if we were to interrupt our work even briefly, we would have to wait until the following year to resume. Reassembling all the workers and equipment would require a great deal of money and effort. Above all, I was concerned that this sort of delay would have a fatal effect on overall morale. But the five hundred workers and staff were undaunted. They were on the brink of achieving what they had earnestly wanted ever since 2003, and none of them complained. Truth be told, their very lives hinged on the success or failure of the canal. Most of the workers had been farmers in the vicinity, and many of them had summoned their families back, believing the project would succeed. If the canal failed, a return to the harsh life of a refugee awaited. Finding themselves on the edge between life and death, they were motivated by a healthy desire to survive.

By late July 2009, the leading edge of the canal had passed the 23-kilometer point and we were within several hundred meters of our target. However, we were prevented from closing the gap by frequent fierce sandstorms that were veritable typhoons of sand; furthermore, workers kept collapsing from heat exhaustion. Even so, they did not let up, and continued their all-out efforts. Our site manager, who had formerly led a guerrilla unit, told me that even during his jihadi days he had never seen such heroism. This is how we managed to finally open the canal on August 3, 2009. The workers were wildly happy; some were in tears.

On August 2, 2009, the leading edge of the canal reached the 23-kilometer mark. The workers are seen here laboring in the burning sands, working toward the target destination.

In February 2010, after we wrapped up our work around the bedrock in the Gamberi Desert, we officially declared the job complete. We invited a few Peshawar-kai representatives to come from Japan and, along with the provincial governor and local government officials whose bailiwicks were affected by our work, we held a celebratory gathering at the mosque and madrassa we had built. We also received a congratulatory telegram from the Japan International Cooperation Agency (JICA), which is devoting energy to the revival of agriculture.

By this time, we had added another 1.2 kilometers to the main Marwarid Canal, so that it now stretched for 24.8 kilometers from Jaribaba in Kunar Province to its final terminus in the Gamberi Desert in Nangarhar. The diversion channels had a total length of 16.7 kilometers. The Marwarid was now carrying 400,000 tons of water per day and irrigating 3,120 hectares of farmland. The facilities we built for irrigation purposes included twelve reservoirs of various sizes, five aqueducts, twelve siphons, one underground water conduit, twenty-six bridges, one set of inlet gates, and thirty-three diversion gates. The ¥1.4 billion in construction costs was covered entirely by the Peshawar-kai from its membership fees and the donations it collected. This was truly a monumental achievement.

Thus, the irrigation canal had been completed. We now entered the next stage of the project: to open the Gamberi Desert to cultivation, maintain the canal, and prepare the water-intake facilities needed for the surrounding region. The casualty record for the project included seven serious injuries (one skull fracture, one rupture of an internal organ, three cases of broken limb bones, and two cases of extremities being crushed). Many people suffered minor injuries that included contusions to the head and body, limb sprains, numerous cuts and abrasions, and probably several hundred cases of heat exhaustion. Only one person died on the job, from a heart attack. Outside of work, two people were kidnapped and murdered, and three others died in drowning accidents.

The tale of the subsequent hardships experienced in opening the desert I will leave for another time. The effort has moved steadily forward as people do battle with sandstorms and floods, and continues to the present day.

A Miracle in the Desert

Four years later, gentle sounds now fill the woods in the Gamberi Desert. Pleasant breezes rustle through the trees, songbirds chirp, and you can hear a chorus of frogs in the distance. Tamarisks standing 10 meters tall provide shade, moderate the harsh hot winds and sandstorms, and further spread

On August 3, 2009, water reached the terminus of the cross-desert channel, 23.6 kilometers from the inlet gates.

the workings of life. It is like a different world from the clamorous scene of Afghanistan. The erosion-control forests that run along the Marwarid Canal have helped make it possible to bring vast tracts of land under cultivation. Our project to create a strip of forest several hundred meters wide by 5 kilometers long—including 200,000 trees for erosion control alone—is finally having an effect. This is a desert no more.

Turning our eyes toward the settlements, we see rich fields spreading before us, and everyone is busy farming. Already 150,000 people have resumed farming in the irrigation canal's watershed, and their lives are returning to stability. This was not something they achieved by sitting idly by. It is the fruition of their combining a healthy desire to survive with great effort and sincere cooperation.

Even more important than building the irrigation canal is maintaining it. At PMS, in addition to deepening the bonds among the people living in the watershed, we have adopted a plan for creating a pioneer village in Gamberi. The goal is to put two hundred local people who worked on the canal project for ten years on the road to self-sufficiency and to allow the skills they cultivated to be passed down for generations to come.

The Marwarid intake weir had been a point of concern. One of the keys to bringing land under cultivation—along with erosion-control forests, which have been growing here for four years—is ensuring there is a stable flow of water going into the canal. Working together with people from the other bank of the canal in Kashkot, we have built a massive continuous weir 505 meters wide in order to stabilize the intake of water.

With this, our efforts to open farmland have been set on a rock-solid foundation. Some 25 kilometers from the turbid waters around the intake weir, the Gamberi plain is peaceful. An immense forest buffer strip protects it from both the sandstorms that could bury cultivated land in sand overnight and from floods that would otherwise swallow houses in an instant. The intense sunlight that led to the deaths of many travelers has now transformed the valley of death into a valley of plenty that promises rich harvests. Thanks to groves of twenty thousand fruit trees, farmland producing massive amounts of grain, vegetable fields, a forest that provides firewood and building materials, and vast meadows for raising livestock in great numbers, it is now possible for people to support themselves living here. With hardly a backward glance at the steadily worsening political situation, the green ground that quietly spreads before us bears wordless witness to the prospect of limitless bounty. Peace is not an idea here; it is reality.

In Psalm 23, David conveys an incorruptible truth that transcends millennia:

The Lord is my shepherd; I shall not want.

He maketh me to lie down in green pastures: he leadeth me beside the still waters.

Yea, though I walk through the valley of the shadow of death, I will fear no evil: for thou art with me. . . .

Surely goodness and mercy shall follow me all the days of my life.

Looking down from a hilltop, the verdant area of human habitation surrounded by the desert presents a magnificent composition of sky, land, and people. The wide erosion-control forest sharply separates the desert from the area of human settlements. People have gathered together to live in this harsh natural setting. This sight of people keeping up their modest existences in the face of nature with its power of life and death gives me a sense of relief and renews my long-held belief: "Heaven is with us." Nature does not speak to us—but it does not deceive us, either. It brings home to us the constant presence of the heavens high above. And it tells us of the abundant blessings that exist regardless of the wretched state of our human world.

Chapter 10

The Lessons of the Great Flood of 2010

Reviving Afghanistan's Eastern Grain Belt and Ensuring Reliable Irrigation

As we drew closer to opening the Marwarid Canal, we began turning our attention to neighboring districts. The wretched conditions in those areas were hard to bear. The drought was now seriously affecting people in many places. Everywhere, farmers were abandoning their villages and becoming refugees.

The irrigation canal created by Peace Japan Medical Services (PMS) mainly promoted the revival of the Sheiwa district, where it helped more than 100,000 people return to farming. However, conditions in the neighboring Behsud and Kama districts remained as desperate as they had been in Sheiwa. The problems in Sheiwa had arisen because people in that district had been drawing water from sources in the Dara-e-Noor valley, and the water they could expect from there had fallen off steeply. We were able to make up for that with water drawn from the mighty Kunar, which allowed us to once again irrigate Sheiwa's parched earth. In contrast, Behsud and Kama were reliant solely on river water for irrigation. While the Kunar River—which draws water from mountains that stand 7,000 meters tall—did not run dry, climate change was making floods more frequent. The existing intake facilities had suffered repeated flood damage, and though they had been repeatedly repaired, their condition steadily deteriorated.

What people in those districts needed was a consistent water supply. Their attempts to grow rice or wheat had been a gamble up to this point. A successful wheat crop depended to a substantial degree on how much rainfall there was in the previous winter, while successfully growing rice required water levels in the river to remain high until early autumn. If conditions fell short, the harvests would be wiped out, Furthermore, there would be conflict among the farmers over whatever water was available. Under such circumstances, no one could be certain of maintaining a decent livelihood. It is impossible to guarantee stable agricultural production if the requisite amount of water cannot be secured when it is needed.

For the intake weirs, we at PMS thought we could build tried-and-true Japanese-style oblique weirs to ensure predictable volumes of water. That said, however much we may talk about irrigation canals as some sort of compromise between human beings and nature, the fact remains that they are human handiwork. An intake weir represents a particularly precarious intersection between the natural world and the human realm. Trying to merge these elements is tantamount to trespassing on sacred ground. In spite of this, we felt that our undertaking would make it possible to revive the ravaged farmlands along the river. We were also confident that using this approach elsewhere would revive other canals and waterways. And so we began our intense efforts with a view to the eventual restoration of the entire grain belt of northern Jalalabad. But the path to establishing a steady supply of water was not to be an easy one.

Creating a Weir to Withstand Both Flood and Drought

I have already spoken of how—after many hardships—we arrived at using the Yamada Weir as our model for use with the Marwarid Canal. Initially, I had thought that raising the level of the water in the river at the intake gate would suffice. My thinking was that if we simply put the weir at an angle it would reduce the pressure of the water passing over it and it would be easier to build. However, I was completely ignorant. Simply extending the jetty at an angle resulted in deep scouring at the tip. The water level of the river was lower the following year—too low to feed into the irrigation canal. In the end, we added more boulders to extend and build up the jetty.

However, the river sank even further the next year, and we were constantly forced to make further improvements and repairs. What I realized later, after seeing an illustrated plan for the Yamada Weir at a local history museum in Asakura, was that our forebears had gone through the same process as we did before they came up with the form of that weir as we know it today.

The plan I saw depicted the situation in 1757, prior to construction of the present Yamada Weir. The intake gate for the Horikawa Canal, an irrigation canal dug in 1663, lay slightly farther downstream, but in 1722 it was moved upstream of the bedrock there to the grounds of Sui Shrine, adjacent to present-day Eso Hachiman Shrine. It seems that this was done in order to increase the irrigated area by putting the intake gate where the water level was higher. People must have thought that intake from the gate would be more consistent if the gate was placed upstream from the natural bedrock, and that the structure would be better able to withstand floods.

Intake Weirs Built by PMS

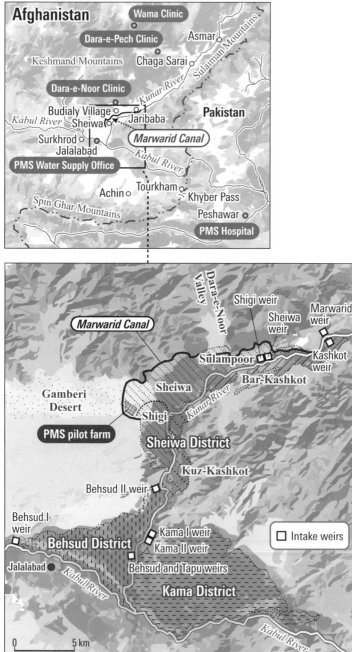

Afghanistan
- Wama Clinic
- Dara-e-Pech Clinic
- Asmar
- Keshmand Mountains
- Chaga Sarai
- Sulaiman Mountains
- Dara-e-Noor Clinic
- Kunar River
- Pakistan
- Budialy Village
- Sheiwa
- Jaribaba
- Kabul River
- Surkhrod
- Jalalabad
- Marwarid Canal
- PMS Water Supply Office
- Kabul River
- Achin
- Tourkham
- Khyber Pass
- Spin Ghar Mountains
- Peshawar
- PMS Hospital

Dara-e-Noor Valley
- Shigi weir
- Sheiwa weir
- Marwarid weir
- Marwarid Canal
- Sulampoor
- Kashkot weir
- Gamberi Desert
- Sheiwa
- Bar-Kashkot
- Kunar River
- Shigi
- PMS pilot farm
- Sheiwa District
- Kuz-Kashkot
- Behsud II weir
- Behsud I weir
- Kama I weir
- Behsud District
- Kama II weir
- Jalalabad
- Behsud and Tapu weirs
- Kabul River
- Kama District
- Kabul River

☐ Intake weirs

0   5 km

Conditions were similar to those we saw in Afghanistan. The places where you can draw water most easily are also the places most susceptible to flooding. The downstream backside of bedrock is the best place to put a weir so as to draw a steady amount of water while avoiding flood damage. This is why we at PMS chose the positions for the Behsud I and Sheiwa weirs as we did. On the other hand, any weir placed on the upstream side of protruding bedrock will be hit by waters of strikingly varied levels. The weir depicted in the illustration appears to be a simple jetty. If the early weir was like this, the riverbed would have subsided due to scouring around the tip of the jetty. That was what we experienced.

The vestiges of an embankment extending into the river from the opposite side at Nakanoshima (as the opposite bank is known) can be seen in the photo of Yamada Weir on page 164. The work done there was to compensate for the effects of the scouring, and it indicates a subsiding riverbed. It seems likely that scouring at the weir's tip, combined with sedimentation within the irrigation canal, gradually blocked the flow of water into the canal.

The simple fact is, the lower the water in the river, the smaller the amount of water that can be drawn into the canal. To address this, our ancestors widened the intake gate here to draw in the amount of water that they needed. According to the documentary record, an intake gate through the bedrock was completed in 1722. However, local residents eventually stopped getting enough water from it for irrigation, and so they expanded it. In 1759 they increased its width from 1.5 meters to 3 meters across, and in 1760 they added 0.9 meters to the height of the weir. These efforts produced a massive increase in the amount of water that could be obtained. What's more, in 1790 they apparently made certain major improvements to the weir that were aimed at keeping the water level constant.

I was particularly interested in the state of the weir before these improvements were made. From a modern history of the weir and canal, *Yamada-zeki/Horikawa sanbyaku-gojū-nen shi* (350 years of the Yamada Weir and the Horikawa Canal), I learned that the weir had repeatedly collapsed or been washed away and was then repaired until it had become something like a jetty built of stone. Because the water flowing over the weir had scoured the area behind it, creating a deep depression, reinforcement of the weir became quite difficult. In short, they were faced with the same problem of scouring at the tip of the jetty and downstream that we were.

Koga Hyakkō, the headman of Asakura village, was the person who expanded the intake gate, designed the stone-pitched weir in its entirety as we know it today, and oversaw the construction project. The illustration presented here captures well the state of the weir before Hyakkō made his improvements.

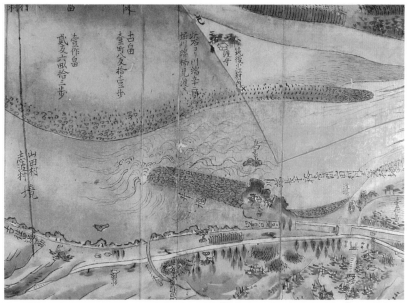

The Yamada Weir section of the *Jōza-gun Geza-gun Ōkawa ezu*. (Illustration of the Ōkawa ["Great River"] in the Jōza and Geza districts.) (Image courtesy of the Amagi History Museum.)

Yamada Weir today. (Image courtesy of the Yamada Weir Land Improvement District.)

It also gives us a way to see what hard work he did. He devoted his entire life to irrigation projects. He was both a superb observer of water and a proficient technician. Following his successful efforts to widen the intake gate, he spent the next thirty years continuing to observe the river. When he was around seventy years old, he roused himself and spent the next three years persuading people from villages in the vicinity—who feared that the excess water might cause damage—to finally allow him to head an effort to create a stone-pitched weir that would raise the level of the entire river. He traveled down almost the same trail of technological improvements that we did.

These water projects need to be seen in the context of the conditions that rural communities faced at the time. The events of the eighteenth century included terrible famines, along with various peasant uprisings, floods, and droughts. The wretched conditions that resulted from the repeated famines left their mark in the form of Buddhist statuary and iconography dedicated specifically to the "Jizō of the starved" bodhisattva that can be found in countless places around Fukuoka. Hyakkō had shared in the joys and sorrows of his villagers struggling with their heavy annual rice tax and the paucity of their diets, and it is safe to say that he probably bet his life on the weir. Building it took more than just technology. Hyakkō is said to have become a devout believer in the Shintō and Buddhist deities, and I am probably not the only one to sense the very human prayers and commitment that imbued the weir. I came to realize that Japan is the way it is today thanks to the ceaseless efforts of people like Hyakkō.

PMS had built an irrigation canal in Afghanistan, but if the weir did not function properly, it would be like having veins with no blood coursing through them. As we made one improvement after another over the years, I gradually came to understand how wonderfully the Yamada Weir operated. To summarize what I learned:

(1) Making the spillway longer allowed better control of fluctuations in water levels (this section measures 309 meters for the Yamada Weir at present, or about four times the width of the natural river channel).

(2) The entire riverbed was raised to prevent scouring.

(3) A sand-flushing ditch was created directly in front of the intake gate to prevent sedimentation in the channel.

(4) All of the river's boulders served to deflect current resistance; stones of various sizes were mixed in among them to create a weir body that would stay together.

(5) The flat surface of the weir was built in a fan shape to concentrate the flow toward the center of the river channel and control its effects on the opposite bank.

The Marwarid intake weir on the Kunar River. (2009.)

The author operating an excavator.

(6) The opposite bank (Nakanoshima) was turned into a flood-control basin to cope with the off chance of overflows.

(7) Branch channels were created upstream to handle major floods.

(8) The intake gates were widened without raising the riverbed more than necessary so farmers could still get enough water even when the river was low.

Based on these design ideas, we made major improvements to the Marwarid weir in 2007 to raise the water level in the river channel in its entirety. The weir could now withstand even the greatest of floods and still function splendidly. The improvement project was massive. The weir was around 300 meters long and 50 meters across at its base, and it took around 2,500 15-ton dump-truck loads of stones to complete. This became our model weir, and its impact helped eventually to revive northern Jalalabad's grain belt. This approach—along with dividing the channels in rivers and canals and our techniques for building embankments—gradually established itself as one of our technologies suited to local conditions.

We built the Sheiwa weir (completed March 2008) and Kama I weir (March 2009) after this. It seemed as though bit by bit we were increasing the amount of land that could be guaranteed a steady supply of irrigation water. However, the final adjustments to our design came about due to an unexpected blow struck by nature.

An Unprecedented Flood

The next major turning point we experienced after the drought of summer 2000 was the great flood of 2010. Much of the rain that falls in an Afghanistan summer takes the form of regionalized downpours that come all at once and very quickly. Any damage they may cause is likewise localized. However, the intermittent rain that was falling on July 28, 2010, was different from usual. The sky was leaden with thick rain clouds that day, and showed no signs of clearing. It had been like that for the past two days. Word had it that the entire eastern side of the Hindu Kush range from Chitral to Kabul was covered with rain clouds, and that in addition to the gentle drizzle, intermittent torrential downpours were also striking across the area. The Kunar River was steadily swelling, and at the Marwarid intake gate it was approaching the highest level ever seen since we began our observations in 2003.

The following morning, I was feeling concerned about the intake gates, and at 10 a.m. we set out on a round of inspections. By this time, PMS had worked not just on the Marwarid intake weir but also on restoring the waterways in the Sheiwa, Kama, and Behsud districts. We regarded the Sheiwa and Kama I intake gates as completed works, and had absolute confidence in them. But I shuddered when I saw the actual conditions at the Kama I intake weir, where water levels had previously been stable. The intake gate itself was completely submerged and there was muddy brown water everywhere. The canal could no longer be distinguished from the river. Astonished, I hurriedly contacted our Marwarid Canal teams and ordered them make sure the intake gates were all closed and the drainage channels were all open. And then I rushed to the canal.

Concentrated Downpours throughout the Gamberi

At 11 a.m., we heard from our crew working in the Gamberi Desert that the canal was being hit there by considerable flooding and they urgently needed instructions on what to do. The problem was at storage reservoir Q2, which sat atop a 16-meter high cliff. The reservoir could hold up to 200,000 cubic meters of water. The worry was about what would happen if the levee burst: a torrent of water would immediately pour out and strike the communities around the village of Shigi downstream. This would be beyond anything we could control. If it resulted in substantial fatalities, it would probably cost me my life as well.

I was there in a flash, and sure enough cascade-like torrents were pouring down from the mountain into the reservoir. I was petrified with fear. I turned pale and stood motionless on the spot. I felt helpless. But human beings are amazing. Once I resigned myself to the impending disaster, I felt impelled by a strange curiosity. I watched the scene with detachment, as if I were observing it from the afterworld, and wondered how the levee would break and fall apart and where its defects were. It was not a matter of being levelheaded nor of being desperate. Whatever it was, I was lost in thought; I do not know for how long. I stared steadily at the leveling rod that showed how high the water was in the reservoir. The level eventually rose about 15 centimeters and then held steady.

In the two years since we had completed the reservoir, the ten thousand trees in the buffer strip had grown to about 5 meters tall. Now, they blunted the force of the water cascading down and provided stout protection for the levee's walls. Our site manager Pacha Gul and my driver Mokhtar were there, and they were both optimistic. "God is with PMS," they kept saying. "Destruction and creation are both God's will."

Later, I learned that the rain in the Gamberi had fallen for around 45 minutes starting at 11 a.m., and the rain from the foothills had flowed into the canal. The storage reservoirs made by blocking off valleys had quickly become swollen, and the water had flowed down along the cliffs to pour into the cross-desert channel. That channel was 5 meters wide and 2.8 kilometers long and could itself hold 20,000 cubic meters of water. It was overflowing everywhere, but most of the excess water washed off into natural floodways. I felt that we had had a narrow escape.

There apparently had been nonstop concentrated downpours across the region around the Keshmand Mountains. The entire Gamberi Desert region—which lay in their southern foothills—was hit by flooding. In particular, at the 800-meter point along the cross-desert portion of the canal, where the land was low, the waters had overflowed and levees had been washed out three times. However, just like at reservoirs Q2 and Q3, the villages downriver were fully protected by the canal. Thanks to the fact that most of the floodwaters had washed into the canal, and furthermore, that the buffer strip of trees had slowed the flow, there were no major disasters. About two years had passed since the riverine buffer strip had been created. It was originally intended to serve as an erosion-control forest, but we now saw that it was having a satisfactory effect in handling floods as well.

Flashboards Break at Sheiwa Weir

With each passing year, owing to changes in the river channel, obtaining water from the existing Sheiwa Canal had grown more difficult. By 2006, the water had completely stopped flowing in the canal, and its watershed was dependent instead on the Marwarid Canal. But with our hopes at PMS to irrigate the Gamberi Desert with phase two of our project, we had ascertained that there would no longer be any surplus water to divert to the Sheiwa watershed in the future. Therefore, we did an enormous amount of work from autumn 2007 to the winter of the following year to bring the Sheiwa Canal back to life. To accomplish this, we first restored around 1 kilometer of the channel and then built an intake weir and gate.

During the 2010 floods, water had flowed over the 4.5-meter-tall intake gate at the Sheiwa weir and left it submerged, albeit by only a few centimeters. However, the bottom flashboard had broken under the pressure, and floodwater had almost gotten in. Meanwhile, the flashboards at the second rank of gates were not in place, and the sliding gates on the drainage channel were closed. These lapses were the fault of the gatekeeper at the time. His excuse was that if he had left the drainage channel open, then the water would have gone to Shetrau village instead of to Sheiwa. By way of explanation, some time before, Sheiwa had sold to Shetrau a huge area of farmland

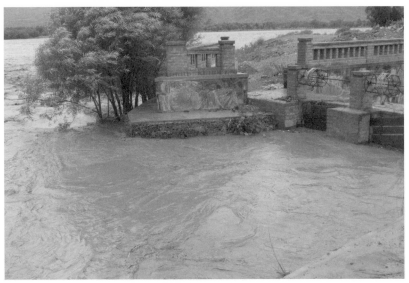

On July 29, 2010, the water level rose rapidly at the Marwarid intake gate due to heavy rains the day before.

The Sheiwa intake gate on the same day.

that was considered unproductive. But after the Marwarid Canal was opened, the farmland had revived and the value of the land had leapt one hundred-fold, from 2,000 rupees to 200,000. Since no one had ever imagined this wasteland would turn into fertile farmland, the people of Sheiwa were envious of their Shetrau neighbors, and there were never-ending conflicts of one sort or another between the two villages.

Water is a resource that must be provided to everyone, regardless of perceived rights or wrongs. I immediately dismissed the keeper and told our staff to put the gate under our direct management. Understandably, there had been a change in the traditional role of the "water keeper" (*miraban*). Generally, getting water is the pressing issue when farming on arid land where little is available, and not much thought was ever given to how to drain it. The people around there also had no concept of adjusting the volume of water. From then on, PMS instituted a practice of directly employing villagers on a rotating basis to serve as gatekeepers; we would then turn management of the gates over to the villagers themselves after they had become versed in how to adjust the water volume.

A Narrow Escape at the Kama Canal

On August 1, a second wave of flooding raised water levels to new heights and swallowed up the riverbanks. Around this time, news stories about these floods began appearing around the world with headlines like, "100 Dead in Nangarhar," "Monsoon Grows to Giant Size, Extreme Rainfall Across Karakoram and Hindu Kush ranges," "10 Million Affected, 1,800 Confirmed Dead in Pakistan—Greatest Disaster Since Country's Founding." Day by day, the number of victims grew. The scope of the calamity was said to be greater than that of the floods of 1929, which had set the previous record. People around the world began offering relief on an enormous scale.

The astonishing thing was that, even amid all this, the Western forces continued their air strikes without a break. We heard that around two dozen refugees who were transporting the dead at a location downstream from the Kama weir were killed in an air raid. It felt like the end of the world was at hand.

Most of the flood's victims on the Afghan side of the border were residents of the Kunar River basin. Significant international support went to Pakistan, but people did not seem to know much about conditions in Afghanistan. The victims I saw here were villagers who had been living close to rivers. In all likelihood, they were people well versed in the old methods for drawing water. Places where you can easily draw water are also places that flood easily. People gave little thought to how to regulate the amount of water flowing in the rivers, and concentrated mainly on how to get water during winter when it was scarce. The Kama district where we wanted to work was no exception.

The limited use of concrete and heavy machinery for river management had, if anything, made the situation worse. The traditional methods involved using sandbags and wood to pile up the weirs. These certainly would be washed away in a flood, but the weir could be rebuilt. However, if you had the means to put down sturdy boulders and create a concrete jetty to raise the water level, you could obtain a large amount of water very quickly. The problem is, such solid structures also generate severe scouring at the tips. As a result, the riverbed falls, and sufficient water for irrigation becomes unavailable during winter, when water is already scarce. Moreover, when there are floods, the water level will rise suddenly, sending massive amounts of floodwater through intake gates that lack the capacity for adjusting water volumes.

To cope with floods, a low levee had been built across part of the main channel in the river to serve as a mechanism for draining off excess water. The idea was not a bad one. However, there was no guarantee that it could drain off the amount of water that a flood might bring. If this type of spillway is weak, it can fall apart, but this will allow the water to pour into natural drainage channels, and damage will still be mitigated. In the Kama district, though, they had had the money to use a lot of concrete in the levee, which created an inflexible structure that conversely was more likely to inflict damage. If more water came in than the system could handle, this sturdy structure would be left standing while the water poured off into the villages. Meanwhile, the area around the tips of the intake weir on this simple jetty grew ever more scoured, causing the riverbed to fall. This seemed to be what had brought these villages to ruin. By 2008, farmers could no longer draw any water from their irrigation canal in winter, and this dealt wheat production a fatal blow.

Around this time, PMS was stepping up its efforts to open the Gamberi Desert and so for financial reasons was reducing its activities in the Kama district. Still, we could not sit idly by and watch the devastation of a region that had once boasted the highest agricultural productivity in eastern Afghanistan. At the Kama II intake gate, where the volume of water could no longer be adjusted, we undertook some temporary measures. However, the work we did was insufficient since it did not extend to drainage facilities.

Now, in August 2010, turbid water was thunderously flowing over the intake gate, and much of it was pouring out along the irrigation canal. The spillway was solid, having been made of sturdy concrete and boulders, but it was too small to drain off the volume of water that this flood was bringing. A vast stream of water had been flowing toward the settlements for hours, and the embankment near the intake gate was already starting to collapse. If we

Before PMS could undertake its planned improvements, the Kama II intake gate was completely inundated by a flood. It was no longer possible to adjust the amount of water flowing through it.

The spillway on the main Kama Canal was incapable of draining off all the water, and so the flood was heading toward human settlements.

did nothing, an even greater flood would pour down into the villages and a horrific tragedy would result.

"Cut off the canal and drain the water!" I cried.

The villagers, in a dither, could only look on. At my urgent instructions an excavator had been hastily brought to the scene, but the operator was hesitant to start working, fearing hostility from the locals. The people of Kama had devoted much thought to the canal, and had paid for it themselves. And it is taboo around here for an outsider to work on the property of strangers. However, PMS was already planning to build a new intake weir and work on the canal that autumn, so I had no hesitation. "Leave it to me," I said. "We'll repair the canal later. Human life comes first!"

I got into the excavator and desperately started hacking away at the spillway. Mokhtar, my driver, grasped the seriousness of the situation. Worried for my safety, he immediately made arrangements to mobilize other heavy machinery in support. "Doctor Sahib, it's dangerous!" he shouted and tried to hold me back. But the other equipment would take at least an hour to arrive, and meanwhile the water was rising right before our eyes. There was no time to spare. The strange thing was that I felt no sense of fear. The reality of it was not tumultuous, like some action scene in a movie. Once I became absorbed in the situation, it was as though I had entered a world of silence. The roar of the flood disappeared and my surroundings grew hushed. Only my willpower and powers of concentration were operating in that sea of mud. All I could think about was my plan of action: If I could use that great stone as a scaffold, and open up that weak-looking part of the levee on the downstream side, then the vehicle would escape from tumbling over. After that, I could head back to the upstream side. I should be able to open a route that would allow the water to escape. This was a battleground. If I did not do something, then many villagers would die. I dug open a 20-plus-meter chunk of the levee, and the muddy waters shifted away from the settlements and flowed off instead toward uninhabited land downstream. And so, thanks to this snap decision, the villages suffered only light damage.

The Marwarid Weir Sandbar Is Washed Away

After the massive improvement project that we undertook in 2007, we had thought we were finished with the Marwarid weir for the time being. It was a sturdy structure that we had packed tight with a great many boulders. The 2010 floodwaters had toppled willow trees on the island in the middle of the river about 160 meters beyond the intake gate, but when I saw the weir on August 1 it was otherwise undamaged and water was not overflowing. So we had been congratulating ourselves. "The weir is fine, and even in a major flood we'll still have room to breathe." "It's fantastic. Now there's a PMS weir for you! Our work is perfect." While other places were exposed to one danger after another, it felt like here was one ray of light. However, as the floodwaters began to ebb, that pride collapsed like a house of cards.

A month later, as the water levels dropped, we saw that something astonishing had happened. The great sandbar to which we had extended the weir had been washed away. This was why there had been no overflows. When the flood passed, it became evident that a new main river channel had opened up where the sandbar had been, and the water for irrigation was no longer flowing over to the intake weir. As a consequence, although it was early autumn, the water had not risen at the intake gate, and the areas alongside the Marwarid Canal were now faced with a grave water shortage. With the autumn harvest at hand, people were growing uneasy. The weir was indeed strong— in fact, it was too strong. Water creates its own channels. The sandbar had been an island 200 meters long and 200 meters wide, covering 40,000 square meters; we never would have guessed that it could completely disappear in those muddy waters to be replaced by the river's new main channel. The technological achievements of humans are only temporary in the face of nature. We had initially escaped disaster by a fluke and were intoxicated by our perceived success. This stunning realization left me unable to act for a while.

But it was a big lesson. My focus shifted from how to make something strong to how to best come to terms with nature. Nature is unpredictable. To understand its logic one must start by letting go of excessive confidence in human technology. It is nature, not humans, that plays the lead role in this drama. Humans are merely picking up its scraps to achieve a modest way of life. I had thought that I already knew this, but it was only when I was faced with this situation that it really hit home for the first time and I understood it deeply. Koga Hyakkō, the builder of the Yamada Weir, had not merely shed tears at the plight of farmers. He also developed a thorough knowledge of nature's furies. He had applied all of his wisdom to the delicate point where human artifice and nature come into contact—and he also applied all his prayers. Speaking of his techniques without mentioning his prayers sells him short.

Establishing a Water Intake System

Thus, these unprecedented floods taught me many lessons. I returned to the starting point in my research on intake weirs and their design. I realized that

I had been gazing at rivers without entirely surrendering my lingering attachment to focusing on humans. I was being called to look thoroughly at human habitations from the river's perspective. It was like the change from the Ptolemaic view of the universe to the Copernican one. You cannot control nature. The benefits we get are nothing other than a reward for our making peace with nature. I was ashamed at my failure to recognize this sooner.

In response to this realization, I reevaluated the entire system for drawing water along the length of the canal, and I made some hypotheses about how floodwater would travel along it. Based on this, I revised the design to incorporate ways to adjust the volume of water flowing down the canal, such as by dividing the waterway into channels and creating embankments and flood-control basins on the opposite bank. The trick we came up with was to make the intake gate as wide as possible so water could be drawn in even when its levels were extremely low. This would avoid generating overflows by raising the weir too high. In addition, we came close to completing our system for keeping sedimentation under control by positioning a sand-flushing ditch in front of the intake gate and then drawing the intake to a sedimentation pond. This brought our work closer to its conclusion.

In March 2010, before the great floods, I was surprised to receive a proposal from the Japan International Cooperation Agency (JICA) asking that Hanazato Nobuhiko, who had just taken up his post as the agency's chief representative in Kabul, be allowed to visit our project site. In September 2009, I had been invited to speak at a hearing in Japan on reconstruction support for Afghanistan. This came just after the administration of Prime Minister Hatoyama Yukio had decided to provide the country an aid package amounting to US$6 billion. In my statement, I eschewed all political discussion and focused only on the drought crisis. I stressed the need to support the restoration of agriculture through reliable irrigation and the importance of achieving food self-sufficiency. JICA's director general for its South Asia Department was interested in what I had to say, and had told Hanazato about it. Hanazato now proposed that he come see the situation for himself. In July, he came to have a look at the Gamberi Desert and the Marwarid Canal. He commented, "This is the first time I've seen a project site where people really are doing the work they say they are." This visit opened his eyes to the straitened circumstances of Afghan farm villages and the importance of having water. I explained to him that it would not be possible to promote agriculture without improving the irrigation system so farmers could cope with the effects of climate change. My advice was that such efforts should be undertaken throughout the country, and that a model project should be implemented in the grain-producing region of northern Jalalabad. Afterward, the security situation deteriorated, and JICA staff could no longer travel around the country. Hanazato was the last Japanese visitor to see the site where we were working.

Still, in addition to completing the Marwarid, Sheiwa, and Kama I weirs on our own, we also wound up collaborating with JICA on a rapid succession of projects, building the Kama II, Behsud, and Kashkot weirs as facilities for drawing water in the surrounding regions. People have various opinions about Japan's official development assistance (ODA), but such trivial political debates were superfluous in the face of the great drought. Furthermore, PMS could not have attempted to undertake such projects on its own across Afghanistan. We did what we could to create practical examples, thinking that if policymakers recognized the value of our work, that should naturally lead to the implementation of more such projects. I felt that what we had accomplished must not end up being an isolated event serving only as the material for a poignant tale.

When the great flood occurred that summer, Hanazato, who was now quite familiar with the situation at our construction sites, cheered us on, saying, "You've turned misfortune into a blessing—your work will make it possible to determine the maximum flood level we need to anticipate." Through extraordinary efforts, he finalized our unusual contract to collaborate. On schedule, that October we began work on the Kama II intake weir and on building the 4-kilometer-long embankment on the opposite bank. After that, the amount of land that could be irrigated steadily increased year after year. Our goal is to revive 16,500 hectares of arable land in the three districts of northern Jalalabad. That will be sufficient to guarantee the livelihoods of around 650,000 farmers while bringing this major grain-producing region back to life.

In March 2013, we finished laying most of the foundations for the Kashkot-Marwarid continuous weir—a project that might well be described as the sum total of a decade's worth of trial and error and hard work. This promised a stable supply of water to irrigate more than 5,000 hectares of land on both sides of the river. That summer, floods that exceeded those of 2010 inundated areas along the Kunar and Kabul rivers several times, but all the intake gates escaped damage. This weir, built to withstand both flood and drought, saved many people. Meanwhile, wet-rice farming has seen intense growth throughout the area affected by our work. This happened because farmers believed they could expect an uninterrupted supply of water. Thanks to the water intake system put in place by PMS, the stable supply of water for irrigation promised locals that they could count on their harvests.

The dream that I have had since 2000, when I first encountered the Yamada Weir in Japan, is now coming true here in Afghanistan.

The completed Kama intake weir.

The intake gate at the Sheiwa weir.

Marwarid-Kashkot Continuous Weir

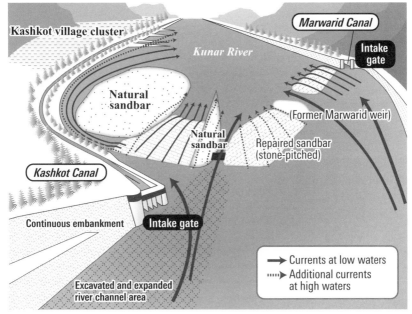

- Kashkot village cluster
- Marwarid Canal
- Intake gate
- Kunar River
- Natural sandbar
- (Former Marwarid weir)
- Natural sandbar
- Repaired sandbar (stone-pitched)
- Kashkot Canal
- Continuous embankment
- Intake gate
- Excavated and expanded river channel area

→ Currents at low waters
⋯▶ Additional currents at high waters

Work was done to divide the river channel so water flows to intake gates on both banks. Here, foundation work is being carried out on an intake gate for the Kashkot Canal.

Conclusion

The End of the War of Retaliation

Sometimes humans are confronted with an unexpected situation that puts them under pressure to make a major decision. Foreign military forces began to withdraw from Afghanistan in July 2011, and in the process of the so-called security transfer to Afghan forces, the country was reaching a turning point. The United States and its allies were bringing a messy end to their direct participation in a conflict that had drawn tens of thousands of their troops into a morass. Amid the chaos of this transitional period, we continued with our project, even though I felt as though we were treading on thin ice. My apprehension was confirmed by an incident on July 17 that truly struck terror in my heart.

That morning, almost none of our staff and workers from Budialy, a village of several thousand inhabitants in the downstream area of the Dara-e-Noor Valley, showed up for work. The women, children, and elderly residents had fled to neighboring villages or to Jalalabad, while the men were tensely watching a fierce encounter unfold. Black smoke rose from the center of their village, around which the US forces had drawn a formidable cordon. The roads were closed and no one could approach.

It was not until evening that we were able to contact people and reports began coming in. Rockets fired from a US base about 30 kilometers away had pulverized the village's school. Apparently, many armed insurgents were killed, and some villagers had been caught up in the chaos. The US forces had also mobilized a large number of troops and helicopters. Many of our workers were trying to learn what had become of their families as they continued to work. However, we were receiving a mixture of real and questionable information that left our work site in an extraordinary state of agitation. When night fell, the darkness made me even more anxious as I speculated about what might lie ahead. Telling myself I must not make any rash decisions or act imprudently, I spent a sleepless night waiting for daybreak.

The local situation seemed to be on the brink of disaster. If the villagers staged an uprising, PMS would be forced to withdraw completely. I braced for the apocalypse that seemed to be coming. I did not want our final chapter to be an ignominious one. I conjectured one gloomy scenario after another. Could I ignore the possible uprising and the prospect that it might lead to casualties among our staff? How would I wrap up our affairs? How would I explain this to our backers in Japan? What would happen to our staff, and what would become of the work we had yet to finish?

The next day, we started to get more accurate information. Only the school had been destroyed. Twenty-seven people were killed; aside from one guard, they were all insurgents—members of the group that had abducted and murdered Itō Kazuya in 2008. The corpse of the ringleader was also identified. The group had been first put together by a foreign road construction company to provide security. It later became closely tied to a locally powerful armed faction and developed into a band that repeatedly engaged in blackmail and assassinations. Its existence had become a deadly nuisance. In the chaos, even anti-government elements made a point of avoiding stirring up any trouble directly with this group. And in some places, it was even in the pay of foreign forces.

After sunset on July 16, the band had attacked the offices of the police and the chief of the Sheiwa district (through which the PMS canal passes), demonstrating that their clout extended to the lower reaches of the Gamberi Desert. After this, they gathered in Budialy, demanded that the villagers feed them, and then billeted themselves in the school. At that point, the men of the village started evacuating the elderly, women, and children. The US forces surprised the group in their sleep with an attack that began around 3 a.m. on July 17. They had been tipped off by the villagers.

He who lives by the sword dies by the sword. This attack sapped the influence of the armed faction to which the group had belonged, and a sense of relief spread throughout the region. However, it was the foreign militaries whose money and weapons had fostered such dangerous groups in the first place. People who had watched the situation closely over the previous decade had complicated feelings—both sympathetic and hostile—toward the group that had met its demise.

One of the dead was a youth I had known. Around ten years old when the air raids began, he had been helping out at a flat-tire repair shop in the bazaar. He was intelligent, with a gentle disposition, and he was a good worker. However, as he grew up, his desire to avenge relatives and his inherent sense of justice led him to become an active participant in attacks on foreign forces. Local sympathy toward him ran deep, and many people joined in his funeral procession. His death was a heart-rending consequence of the decade of airstrikes in Afghanistan. The more I learned about the situation, the more inhuman

I felt it to be. All the Japanese commentary on the Afghan situation now sounded empty to me. The framework of "Western forces versus Taliban" was gone. The only options remaining for Afghans were to either join up with a violent group for money, revenge, or political purposes, or to fight against such groups. People of respectable sensibilities had become fed up with the chaos and no longer expected anything from the political realm. What most farmers wanted was just three meals a day and peace in their hometowns.

The terrible incident was over in a day. It was time for me to put my doubts behind me and get back to my proper job. We continued to work diligently on the PMS irrigation project as though this dispiriting incident had been just a dream. Our crew of four hundred people was standing up to the ferocity of nature in a desert that blazed with temperatures exceeding 50°C and alongside a great river that swirled with muddy water. Even though living there was difficult and we were plagued by sandstorms, droughts, and floods, the power of hope made it possible for them to carry on with their work. Though I lack the words to describe their commitment properly, they were in high spirits knowing that their labor would help their families and hometowns.

Humans do not live merely to eat. The completion of all of the intake gates we were working on for the Kashkot and Behsud districts would revive the northern Jalalabad grain belt and safeguard the livelihoods of many farmers. They knew that, and it encouraged them.

Catastrophe and Hope

International interest in Afghanistan's reconstruction gradually faded, and the subject disappeared from the world news. Aside from reports about the fighting or political developments, the occasional articles that did appear were somber items about the deteriorating security situation. In fact, after the International Red Cross withdrew following an attack on their offices in Jalalabad in May 2013, PMS was the only foreign organization working in eastern Afghanistan. We had gone back to where we began. In fact, the situation was even worse than before, as we were on our own.

It pains me to discuss the outcomes of the armed intervention from the "War on Terror" and the enormous amount of financial support that was provided. Thousands of foreign troops were killed in action. Thousands more suffered psychological damage, resulting in suicides and harm to others. Security was at its worst, and the political situation was close to anarchy. The drought continued to generate refugees and make people jobless in vast numbers, while terrorist attacks and accidental air strikes were causing countless fatalities.

Plotting and sabotage had become everyday affairs; the International Security Assistance Force (ISAF) began its troop withdrawals, and the transfer of responsibility for security to Afghan government forces continued. The resistance forces were also in a state of disarray. It seemed as though the foreign forces were trying to avoid direct conflict and were instead engaging in plots to stir up needless internal discord. People succumbed to paranoia, feeling that they no longer had any authority in which they could trust. The developments in the political sphere were cause for despair.

Coincidentally, news of the 2011 Tōhoku earthquake, tsunami, and nuclear disaster in Japan reached us just as our canal project was cleaning up after the great flood. Nature's ferocity had once again claimed many victims, and the disaster also stirred up memories of the dangers of nuclear power. Japan itself also seemed to be at a major turning point. However, the situation as it developed in the aftermath was quite discouraging. I felt as though Afghanistan was not the only place whose people had been abandoned. Japanese society, as always, was concerned with economic growth, and it continued to operate under the illusion that this was the key to solving all problems. Supposedly, only a strong economy could relieve the hardship suffered by victims of the disaster. Meanwhile, politicians were saying that Japan's ideal of peace as a national policy must be reconsidered. This is the dangerous fantasy of people who know war only in the abstract. War is not a game. I can bear witness to that with certainty from my experience in Afghanistan.

When I think of conditions in Japan—where people depend on a risky form of electrical power and where society is rife with uncertainty and instability—I cannot brush off such matters as someone else's problem. But the age of using violence and untruths to preserve short-term profits is working to bring about its own destruction. People have never been reexamining the relationship between nature and humanity from the ground up as earnestly as they are now. It certainly is not an age without hope. But we must not let ourselves be deluded by the products of human effort that stand separate from nature; instead we must strive to recognize the blessings that nature has given to us. Our survival hinges on the quest to open up the limitless frontier that these blessings offer us.

Becoming Divorced from Nature

A peculiar sense of alienation suddenly comes over me whenever I return from Afghanistan to Japan. I keep asking myself why that is. The country seems tidy and clean, and the people going hither and yon seem sophisticated. I sense nothing boorish or vulgar. Nor need I endure dust, the roar of heavy machinery, conflicts over water, people facing starvation, or the need to protect myself from flying bullets. The young people and the women strolling the elegant streets in their choice of fashionable attire catch my eye. Japan is a peaceful country. But I feel that something is lacking.

I remove myself from the hustle and bustle of the city streets and head into the mountains where I played as a child. Japan is a beautiful country, like a dream. The plains visible through my car windows are carpeted with fields and rice paddies as far as the eye can see, and both the distant mountains and the levees along the rivers are covered with verdant woods. In the spring, after I have tramped over the fallen leaves and headed into the mountains, I am greeted by cherry blossoms in full bloom and the brilliance of fresh green foliage starting to bud. The roads have been improved, but the setting that greets me in the depths of the mountains is the same as it was fifty years ago.

If there is anything that makes me feel nostalgic, it is the memories of my encounters with nature and the people that I knew in my childhood. However, when I try to substantiate those memories, I find the past that has been embellished in my mind no longer conforms to reality. I recall the mountains where I would dash about with my insect-collecting net in hand; I recall the individual trees; I even recall the cowpats on the side of the paths. And these memories all bring me back to how gazing at the activities of insects made my heart pound. Today, there is no dirt on the paved road that goes deep into the mountains; cars, rather than cattle and horses, travel along it.

In both city and country, I sense a decisive severing from the world of my nostalgia. Today's world has lost its human aura. And nature has become a subject for commentary and photography; it is no longer something that directly inspires fear, surprise, and delight. We have been placed on something like a conveyor belt, and we can be aware of nature only as scenery that passes by outside our car windows. We are growing ever more distant from real nature. The more the media increases our knowledge of nature with its digital imagery, the farther the reality recedes from us.

To put it in extreme terms, our technological civilization itself is an enormous activity that creates barriers between ourselves and nature. We are living under the delusion that we can even bring time and natural phenomena under our control. Never before have we been able to acquire knowledge and information as readily or to get around as quickly as we can now. When I think of how things were just a few decades ago, I sense that we are living in an entirely new age. However, there is no guarantee that increasing your knowledge will make you any wiser. I cannot help feeling that the advances in the distribution of information and the means of transportation are causing us to get caught up in matters of no consequence and leading to an increase in unnatural developments. I hope that this is just me overthinking things.

The Restaurant of Many Orders

Miyazawa Kenji wrote a children's story nearly a century ago called "The Restaurant of Many Orders" that predicted our time.[1]

It begins with the appearance of two gentlemen dressed in Western fashion who have come from Tokyo to hunt. They are shouldering shiny firearms and accompanied by two great bear-like white dogs. But they become separated from their local guide, a professional hunter, and lose their way, and then the dogs suddenly collapse. They bemoan their great loss, and then, just as they are becoming uneasy with hunger, a magnificent Western-style edifice appears before them. Feeling that they have been saved, they approach and are delighted to see a sign that reads, "Restaurant: Wild Cat House." They go inside, and there see a sign written in stately gold letters, "Anyone may come in. Plump and young customers especially welcome." They advance along the corridor to see another sign that reads, "Please bear in mind that this is a restaurant of many orders." Thinking that the menu must certainly be ample, they proceed further, and as if by magic, a series of instructions in gold letters appears before them: "Tidy yourself up and wipe off any mud," "Take off anything metal," "Spread cream on your face, hands, and feet," and finally, "Rub salt over your body." At this point, they realize it is not the customers who do the ordering but rather whoever is on the other side of the door. They can hear from beyond the door the voices of the wildcats who are preparing to cook the customers.

They regret having entered this awful place, and they are paralyzed with fear and horror. Then the dogs suddenly burst in, barking and growling, and there is a great commotion. The room disappears in a puff of smoke and they find themselves in an empty forest. The clothing they had taken off and the things they carried are scattered around the trees, and they are naked and shivering. Their guide, dressed rustically in a straw raincoat, comes up calling, "Gentlemen! Gentlemen!" and rescues them. He gives them dumplings to eat, and they feel safe at last.

This story is filled with elements that lampoon today's Japan. We are

---

1   The summary that follows is paraphrased from John Bester's translation of Miyazawa's story. The tale is included in *Once and Forever: The Tales of Miyazawa Kenji* (New York Review Books, 2018), a collection of stories translated by Bester.

naturally enticed by "gold letters," and we follow instructions. A building that is beautiful at first sight further deepens our confidence. However, when it comes to what lies beyond its doors, no one truly knows. Our ignorance is by no means limited to the situation in Afghanistan; indeed, our worldview and things that we consider common knowledge are frequently built on fictions.

People are easily deceived by artificial fancies. We are frightened at the shadows of illusory uncertainties. And we think of rustic hunters and their dumplings as unfashionable. Fabrications summon more fabrications, and our worries, swollen by our notions, turn into realities. The more we possess, the more we are dominated by our concerns and feelings of defensiveness. It is a vicious cycle.

War and Peace

As I said at the beginning of this book, the issues of war and peace have been present in my life since I was young. The deaths of my father's relatives in the massive air raid on Fukuoka; the suicide of my uncle Hino Ashihei, driven to despair at being called a "war writer"; the visit of a nuclear-powered US aircraft carrier to Kyushu in my university days—through developments like these, the US military stubbornly kept turning up in my life. But never, even in my dreams, would I have thought that these armed forces would follow me to Afghanistan.

Now, when I see harbingers of military conflict in the world and a social climate in Japan where brash rhetoric runs rampant and people might even approve the use of armed force, I am left speechless. The voices of those calling for peace are becoming ever more muffled.

However, there is one thing I can be certain of from my experiences in Afghanistan: I was never protected by military might. Defense does not necessarily depend on weapons. When our Dara-e-Noor clinic came under attack in 1992, I ordered our people not to shoot even if we suffered fatalities. By preventing a cycle of retaliatory killing, we created a bond of trust that protected us and our work thereafter. If you are a soldier who has been exposed to battle, you know that not firing your weapon requires greater courage than firing it.

The construction sites in farm villages where we work today are in places that have long been regarded as danger zones. However, except for the roads, these sites are safer than anywhere else. PMS's security guarantee is the trusting relationship we have with the local population. If we are regarded as true friends, the locals will spare no effort to protect us.

Trust is not something that is built in a day. The way to touch people's hearts is by showing the sincerity to look beyond personal interests, to practice patience, and to not retaliate with deception even when deceived. This path provides solid security greater than what military might can provide, and it can move people. For us, peace is not an idea—it is real power. We talk with too much ease about war and peace. I believe we should give some quiet thought as to what exactly can be protected by the use of force and what it is that we really should be protecting.

Immutability and Fluidity: What Changes and What Does Not

If we look around today, we will find ourselves surrounded with an abundance of easy ways to enjoy ourselves and forget our anxieties. We are also surrounded by "voices of authority" great and small. We have easily fallen prey to such voices in the past, as have other countries around the world. The ostensibly brave tenor of talk about "not backing down from a war" and the push toward violence in the international community are examples of such voices. How foolish people are when they sacrifice peace for the sake of economic interests, when they look with disdain at another nation, calling it "undemocratic" and "backward," when they show rage over territorial disputes involving tiny slivers of land, and when they believe that an economic recovery will bring happiness. Human happiness lies in another dimension.

Human beings truly do not need much. At the very least, I am free from the notion that you can do anything and be happy if you have money, and from the blind belief that military might alone can protect me. What is true, what is superfluous, and what at minimum is common to all of us as people—we should look closely at questions like these, take a hard look at ourselves, and try to restore a healthy relationship between our feelings and nature.

For sixty-eight years since the end of World War II, I have lived in the spiritual atmosphere of the times, just like other Japanese. When I was growing up, the members of the Meiji generation (born 1868–1912) were gradually receding into the past, but they continued to be a vigorous presence; the core of Japanese society consisted of people who had lived through the ravages of World War II. Japan's culture and traditions, our pride as Japanese people, and our enthusiasm to be reborn as a nation of peace—things that have to some degree faded today—colored that era. At the time we believed that we could avoid future tragedy if we stuck to the postwar paradigm. However, as I look at conditions today, I am struck by the contrast between then and now. For all the talk of "progress" and "reform," it seems to me that Japan has turned into a terribly constrained and cramped place.

Nonetheless, the things that are immutable remain so. It was probably the same hundreds of years ago during the Edo period and thousands of years ago during the Jōmon period. We must not be needlessly carried away by the current of the times and lose sight of what is important, or allow ourselves to be shackled by the magic word "progress," or treat life carelessly. The reality of the "reform" and "progress" touted by today's adults resembles the magic trick in which a magician casts a rope up into the air and then climbs it. We must not be fooled. It was a child unconcerned about appearances, unencumbered by preconceptions, and unfettered by conflicting interests who cried out, "The emperor has no clothes!" I have hopes for the younger generation.

"Heaven is with us"—that one thread running through this book is an ironclad certainty that has supported me solidly from the bottom up. Ultimately, a Tower of Babel that stands isolated from nature will fall. Humans are part of nature. This reality is a blessing, an unshakable element of providence that exists within humans as well and governs the workings of life. Unless human activities in every realm—be it science or economics, medicine or farming—are directed toward seeking compromises between nature and humans, and among humans themselves, there will be no way for humans to survive. This is the orientation of a proper civilization. Even though the calls for such an approach may be a faint murmur underground now, before long our present era will be called to account, and the stream will emerge and gather strength, inevitably developing into a mighty current.

That is my message, the unadorned conclusion that I have reached after thirty years of working in Afghanistan.

The Dr. Nakamura Tetsu I Knew

Yatsu Kenji
Nihon Denpa News Co., Ltd.

It is December 5, 2019. U2—one of the greatest rock bands in the world—is playing a concert in Japan. The arena is packed with close to thirty thousand rapturous fans. The band takes to the stage with one of their signature numbers, "Sunday Bloody Sunday." The lead singer, Bono, grabs the audience's attention right away with his impassioned singing. Then, just a few songs into the show, in the middle of a song called "Bad," he suddenly starts calling out a Japanese person's name and offers words of praise.

"Can we take a moment in the dark," he calls out to the audience, "just to notice that we're here? That we're present, that we're together. Let's see some indoor starlight. . . . Let's turn this sports stadium into a cathedral. Let's turn our phones into candles. Let's take a moment to memorialize the great Tetsu Nakamura. For Tetsu Nakamura. Peshawar-kai! A great man, a great generous person."

When the song draws to an end, Bono again invokes the name, shouting, "For Tetsu Nakamura. . . . Blessed are the peacemakers!" As he does so, the band breaks into another of their signature songs, "Pride (In the Name of Love)." That song is dedicated to the American civil rights leader Dr. Martin Luther King, Jr., who was assassinated in 1968.

> One man come in the name of love
> One man come and go
> One man come he to justify
> One man to overthrow. . . .
>
> Free at last, they took your life
> They could not take your pride
>
> — U2, "Pride (In the Name of Love)"

On that day in 2019, U2 superimposed over its tribute to the life of Dr. King a tribute to this "Tetsu Nakamura." That man is, of course, the author of this book, Dr. Nakamura Tetsu. He spent thirty-five years in Afghanistan and Pakistan, where he directed a nonprofit organization that provided medical care to communities in remote mountain areas, and later went on to build the Marwarid irrigation canal. The day before the U2 concert, he was gunned down and killed in Jalalabad, Afghanistan, by unknown parties. The tragic news quickly spread around Japan and the world; it had reached the band, too, leading Bono to offer an impromptu memorial in the middle of their show.

What sort of person was Dr. Nakamura that not only Japanese and Afghans but an internationally famous band like U2 would be moved to pay him tribute? What did he do, and what did he leave behind? If you read the autobiographical account he presents in this book, I think you will get a full understanding of his thinking and how he put his ideas and beliefs into practice.

As a documentary cameraman, I filmed Dr. Nakamura's activities in Afghanistan for twenty-one years from 1998 to 2019, and used that footage in making several documentary television programs and movies. But over the long years of my association with him, I stopped thinking of him as someone I was filming professionally; instead, I came to look up to him as my life mentor, the guide in whose footsteps I was striving to follow.

To be sure, Dr. Nakamura was a giant of our time, and I cannot possibly present a full picture of him in just these few pages. So in what follows I will focus on four characteristics that I think are important for understanding him based on what I observed during the twenty-one years I trailed him. He was a man of integrity who lived altruistically, a person of exceptional intellect, a righteously brave man, and a man of benevolence who believed every human being is worthy of love.

Each of these four dimensions of Dr. Nakamura's character deserves deep consideration, and I cannot present them properly in a few simple words. But it is my mission to tell others about Dr. Nakamura, and so I will do my best to describe the man I saw and knew.

A Man of Integrity Who Lived Altruistically

On December 4, 2019, while I was conducting an interview in Tokyo, my mobile phone started vibrating like mad with call and text notifications. I ignored the distractions and concentrated on the interview, but when it was over and I was finally able to look at my phone, I saw messages from my colleagues and friends with the unthinkable news that something had happened to Dr. Nakamura.

"Dr. Nakamura was shot by unknown persons in Jalalabad, Afghanistan," read one. "He was severely wounded, but he narrowly escaped death," said another. "The perpetrators fled and have not been arrested," said a third.

I remember feeling shocked. My vision blurred and my mind went blank. I could only hope and pray that at least his life would be spared. But those hopes were dashed a few hours later by a television news flash: "Dr. Nakamura Tetsu was shot on the outskirts of Jalalabad, Nangarhar Province, Afghanistan. He received emergency care at a local hospital, but died while being transferred to hospital in the capital, Kabul."

I could not believe it was real. I could not even shed tears at that moment. All I could think was, "Who took Dr. Nakamura's life? Why was his life taken away?" It was not that I wanted to go looking for the perpetrators myself. Even if they were caught, it would not bring him back to life. I was seized by the horrifying thought that perhaps in a way we had all taken his life: we knew that the war in Afghanistan was still going on, but we were apathetic because it was so far away; we looked the other way as people stripped of their dignity were suffering from poverty and discrimination; and we failed to take the effects of climate change, like drought, seriously in the way he did.

If we had all given more thought to Afghanistan and given it the support it truly needed, then perhaps the security situation might have improved. And if that had happened, then perhaps Dr. Nakamura would not have lost his life. He had confronted all of these problems very seriously and shouldered them as an ongoing personal burden.

That evening, I spent a long time looking at a photograph of Dr. Nakamura that I had taken in Afghanistan. In it, he smiles peacefully and gently against the backdrop of a verdant landscape restored by water from the Marwarid Canal he built. As I stared at the photo I was beset by deep sadness, and suddenly my tears began to flow. He truly was a gentle and peaceful man. He spoke haltingly and gently, not only in everyday conversation, but even when he was issuing directions at the canal work site. He was a contemplative sort of person, one who rarely raised his voice.

However, he was also a man of many dimensions. He had rock-hard determination, great powers of discernment, an exceptional intellect, and rare courage. When he was interacting with patients in his role as a physician and at critical moments on the work site, he displayed a piercing gaze that hinted at the keen power within, and his lips would be tightly drawn. No matter where he went or whom he met, his attitude toward others was always the same, and he dealt with everyone impartially and kindly. He did not boast or brag. When he spoke about Afghanistan, he would mostly restrict his comments to his work and not mention any of his personal experiences. He was always on the side of those who were vulnerable. He loved people and lived for others—he was someone you would describe as a "righteous man." Following his conscience, he lived for others with no regard for himself. He placed absolute value on such behavior.

I have a vivid memory of a moment in March 2008, four years after water had first been sent down the Marwarid Canal; construction was still underway. I was standing with Dr. Nakamura atop a low hill alongside the canal. Spread out before us was the green expanse of a wheat field that had begun to revive thanks to water from the canal. He remained silent as he gazed intently at the scene before his eyes.

At that moment, I turned my video camera on him and caught the look on his face. Through the viewfinder, I could see that it bore an expression that suggested he had reached some deep understanding. After I stopped filming, Dr. Nakamura began to speak: "The farther we extend the canal, the greater the expanse of green becomes. And people truly rejoice at our progress. The more we do, the happier they are. What work could be better than this? I'm lucky to have been able to make this my job."

Dr. Nakamura received no monetary compensation for his aid work. For thirty-five years, he did it all free of charge. I heard that in the earlier years he supported his family with income he earned by working as a physician at a friend's hospital whenever he was back in Japan. Once construction of the Marwarid Canal began in 2003, the project kept him too busy to keep doing that work. I understand that his only source of income after that was from the fees that he received for giving lectures during trips to Japan. He would be invited from time to time to participate in meetings where he could tell people what conditions were like in Afghanistan.

One of the many things I learned from Dr. Nakamura was the meaning of work. Why do people work? By observing him I learned the answer: the essence lies in working for others. He was a true altruist.

The province of Nangarhar in eastern Afghanistan, where Dr. Nakamura was based, was once a fertile region, and it was known as a grain belt. But its climate has always been harsh. In the summer, temperatures rise to nearly 50ºC. This is in sharp contrast with the winter, when day after chilly day, the temperature rises no higher than 10ºC. Furthermore, as described in this book, a terrible drought that struck the region in 2000 turned environmental conditions deadly.

Dr. Nakamura lived in Jalalabad, the provincial capital, for nearly thirty years. His life must have been hard, both physically and psychologically. His daytime activities took him outdoors, and in summertime he would sweat in the blistering heat. The area where the canal work was being done was mostly wasteland with virtually no trees and no place to escape the rays of the sun.

He would tax his body every day from morning until mid-afternoon. Once, he told me with a smile, "The summers here are truly hot. Even so, all the Afghans stoically carry on with their work without a word of complaint. If I were to grumble, the reputation of Japanese men would go out the window."

After the day's work was done, he would return to his lodgings. There was no family waiting for him there, nor the warm bath favored by Japanese custom. He had an old air conditioner in his room that rattled when it was on. But Jalalabad had extended power outages at times, and I imagine he experienced many sleepless nights because of the heat.

The meals that sustained him physically were quite frugal. For breakfast, he had naan flatbread with honey and either English or Japanese tea. He would eat one of the lunches delivered to the work site, joining his Afghan staff under a modest tent. He consumed basically the same thing for lunch every day: one naan and a soup of vegetables simmered with tomatoes. Having tea after a meal was one of the Afghans' few pleasures; they liked to drink their green tea with lots of sugar in it. Dr. Nakamura would add just a little sugar to his tea; then he would squeeze some lemon into it. His dinner generally consisted of the same sort of tomato soup he had had for lunch along with rice that he steamed himself. Occasionally, he would add some mutton to the soup. On days off, for a change of pace he would eat instant ramen or something else that he had brought back from Japan. On those occasions, he would say with a big grin, "Today I'm having a feast!" He was truly single-minded in his lack of regard for himself in the midst of his dedication to others.

A Person of Exceptional Intellect

You might think Dr. Nakamura would have relaxed after finishing one of his frugal dinners, but that was never the case. Every evening, he would hole up in his room and continue to study. When I was in Afghanistan on reporting trips, I would stay in the room next to his. If I got up during the night to go to the bathroom, when I stepped out into the corridor I would almost invariably see light leaking out from the cracks of the door to his room. He cut down on sleep to study and draw up blueprints, and he was constantly thinking about the canal project.

During the years the Marwarid Canal was being built, Dr. Nakamura worked extremely hard to build up his knowledge of civil engineering, a field that lay completely out of his areas of expertise. Constructing a canal involves more than just digging a ditch and letting the water flow. It requires a difficult excavation process in which you take precise measurements and create a slope based on those numbers. On this project, the slope was a drop of 12 centimeters for every 100 meters of canal, and it called for delicate work. Dr. Nakamura essentially went back to school again, teaching himself to handle everything from designing the canal to actually building it. Mathematics, physics, fluid mechanics—he read specialized texts, solicited opinions from experts, and absorbed knowledge about these and other subjects related to civil engineering. His efforts were staggering.

Some might wonder whether a physician could really master civil engineering theory and techniques just by teaching himself. But in fact, through hard study and his superb innate aptitude, Dr. Nakamura did just that. Every single day he would put what he had learned into practice on the job site, and through trial and error he acquired genuine skills. Likewise, when he was working on the construction of a mosque, he taught himself how to create blueprints and carry out structural calculations. He also drew pictures of the structures when the canal work was underway. He could draw them precisely, replicating their distinctive features on paper with no superfluous lines.

Incidentally, he began his career in medicine as a psychiatrist. Many other physicians lauded him for his skills and for his depth of knowledge as a neurologist. I felt that he must be a Leonardo da Vinci–level genius to have such a remarkable series of heaven-sent talents.

While leading his grueling lifestyle, Dr. Nakamura limited his pleasures to reading and listening to Mozart in his room. And when he was outdoors, he would occasionally stop in the middle of his hard work to observe butterflies and insects that happened to catch his eye. I once had a conversation with him about classical music. I recall mentioning that I liked Beethoven. He responded, "I prefer music that eases my mood and makes me feel free. Beethoven is a great composer, but his music is heavy and doesn't put me at ease. Mozart is better in that respect. As a composer, he carefully considered how to deliver sounds that would produce joy in people's hearts. It doesn't matter which of his pieces I listen to; he always lifts my spirits."

From time to time, Dr. Nakamura would offer me a cup of coffee in his room, and we would enjoy some chitchat. I would nearly always see some book he was in the middle of reading lying facedown on his desk. Sometimes it was *Records of the Grand Historian*, a Chinese classic from the first century BC; or it might be *The Analects of Confucius*; or maybe *Man's Search for Meaning* by Austrian psychiatrist Viktor Frankl. Dr. Nakamura was a true intellectual who attentively reread many classic works. He would convey what he meant to say by citing words and deeds taken from the world's classic texts and thinkers, quoting them nonchalantly in his remarks. Conversations with him were peppered with comments like, "It's reported that at this time the

Jacobin Robespierre said such-and-such," "I think the theologian Karl Barth understood that to be like this," or "Considering that this is based on Viktor Frankl's experience. . . ." As for me, I could recognize the name "Robespierre" and I knew that he was a political figure from French history, but that was it. Being able to quote his words in casual conversation requires first having read an enormous number of books and then being able to remember what those books said. Moreover, Dr. Nakamura absolutely never flaunted his exceptional intellect. You could sense that his accumulated knowledge lay behind the things he said. That, combined with the firm cadence of his words, got through to the soul of the person listening.

A Righteously Brave Man

Climate change is said to be the chief culprit behind the drought that has afflicted Afghanistan. This phenomenon has had a complex effect on the country's environment. Dr. Nakamura discusses the situation in detail in this book, but let me give a quick explanation here: In past years, the snow that accumulated in winter atop the country's 4,000-meter-high peaks would melt off bit by bit over the course of the year, yielding water that could be used for the farmlands at the base of the mountains. But the warming produced by climate change meant that temperatures began to rise very rapidly in spring. The accumulated snow thus began melting just as suddenly, dumping a large volume of water into rivers and causing floods. Furthermore, despite the drought, there were also massive localized downpours; those, too, would sometimes result in great floods. Eastern Afghanistan today faces the paradoxical reality of drought and floods occurring in the same place.

In July 2010, Dr. Nakamura saw firsthand what could happen as a result of climate change. Picture the scene: The raging waters of the Kunar River are cascading before his eyes. That swollen mass of brown water surges past him without letting up until, in no time at all, it has all drained off. The intake gates he had been working on have already been swallowed up by the waters. On July 27, the rain that had been falling since before dawn gradually increased in intensity and turned into an off-and-on torrential downpour. The entire region from western Pakistan to eastern Afghanistan was hit by rains of the sort seen only once every few decades. The mountains around Jalalabad were also being hit by those rains, and the water that accumulated traveled through countless valleys before it eventually poured into the Kunar River. The amount was increasing with every passing minute, and there were no signs that its intensity would let up. Dr. Nakamura anticipated this would produce flooding, and together with Mokhtar—his Afghan driver from Peace Japan Medical Services (PMS)—he hastened to the place where work was being done on a canal for the Kama district. Later on, Mokhtar told me what happened next:

Dr. Nakamura stood on somewhat higher ground in the pouring rain with no umbrella and stared intently at the waters that had swallowed up the intake gate. After a while, he spoke to me. "Get me an excavator."

I didn't understand what he wanted to do, and I was confused. I asked him, "What will you do with an excavator in those waters?" I couldn't believe my ears when he answered, "We need to destroy part of the canal so at least some of the water can escape. Otherwise an enormous amount of water will travel down the canal, and it might flow into the villages downstream and destroy them."

Right at that moment the canal was engulfed by the torrent, and you could hardly tell it apart from the river. Anyone going in with an excavator would surely be swept away. I protested, "Please don't. It's too risky to go into the river under conditions like this." But he said, "If I don't act now, the villages downstream will be in danger. I won't regret it, even if I lose my life. If I don't help Afghanistan now, when will I help it? I'm willing to die for the canal and the villagers. There's no point unless I do it now. Let's get to it."

At that moment, I realized that he was truly ready to die, and that he wouldn't change his mind even if I tried to stop him. We went into the water together, and he worked the excavator to cut an opening in the canal wall. The villagers who were watching us got inner tubes and made ready in case the two of us got washed away.

Incidents like this showing Dr. Nakamura's righteous bravery are too numerous to list. Allow me to describe just one more. This happened around thirty years ago, and it left a lasting impression on the staff at PMS's Dara-e-Noor clinic. The clinic was a lifesaver for the people who lived in that mountainous region of Afghanistan with little access to medical care. Every day, many villagers would come in the hope of receiving treatment. Everyone kept their place in line as they awaited examination. But on this occasion, a local strongman ignored the line and forcibly demanded an examination right away on behalf of a relative seeking to consult with the doctor. (Bear in mind that Afghanistan at the time had yet to see any adequate attempts at disarmament, so he was easily able to outfit his men with small arms.) Undeterred, Dr. Nakamura stood firm in the face of this line-jumping and refused. The strongman then summoned his underlings, who were armed with rifles; they surrounded the clinic and shot it up.

Some of the staff members being shot at were farmers who had once been guerrilla fighters themselves. They started getting their own weapons together and prepared to return fire. Even today, the staff still talk about what Dr. Nakamura did next to bring the situation under control. "Don't fire a single shot back—not one!" he said. His subordinates protested, "But they fired on us! Can't we even fire one shot in return?" The doctor replied, "Don't return fire, even if it means we get killed. Who's going to suffer if you shoot back and it develops into a gunfight? It's all the sick people around here. If this turns into a shootout, our clinic won't survive." His courageous refusal to return fire surprised the Afghans, friend and foe alike, and as a result the conflict was quelled.

Dr. Nakamura would take action regardless of the risk to himself. And his actions were backed up by his strong-minded determination. Afghan men set great value on such righteously brave behavior. For them, calling a man courageous is the highest form of praise. Afghans who saw his courage up close fell under his spell and followed him. In Afghanistan, the leaders of large organizations generally do not turn up at the sites where their underlings work. The image of a leader there is a person who issues directions from luxurious, air-conditioned rooms. But Dr. Nakamura spent all of his time working outdoors. Whether in blistering heat or with cold winds blowing, he would be out there side by side with the workers, carrying stones, getting dusty, wielding a shovel, operating heavy machinery, or sitting on the ground eating his meal.

A Man of Benevolence Who Believed Every Human Being Is Worthy of Love

This scene took place twenty-one years ago, in 1998, on my first trip to film Dr. Nakamura. Somewhere in the mountains along the Afghanistan-Pakistan border, I was being jolted about on horseback as I gazed at Dr. Nakamura atop his own steed ahead of me. He was dressed in distinctly unimpressive work clothes; on his head was a well-worn hat of the local variety. He had a moustache and a sparse, unshaven beard, and he spoke rather falteringly, with his eyes half-closed. "What kind of person is this?" I wondered. I was having a hard time figuring him out. He had fastened medical equipment, medicine, a tent, and a sleeping bag to his horse's back. We were riding as part of a clinic caravan heading to a district in the highlands where the villages lacked medical services. He said little as he rode along, swaying atop his horse.

But when we reached a village in those highlands at an altitude close to 4,000 meters, I glimpsed one aspect of what made this man so impressive. Word had gotten around to the neighboring villages that a doctor was coming, and a stream of people had crossed mountains and valleys to gather here. When he started his examinations, his eyes quickly filled with energy and his expression changed. He had stacked up medicine chests to create an examination table, and he worked without taking any breaks at all. He even did surgery inside the tent, relying on a headlamp for illumination.

This was the picture that Dr. Nakamura presented as he worked hard to provide the best possible medical care under field-hospital-like conditions. He displayed powerful affection and deep understanding toward these needy people. In return, the mountain villagers demonstrated feelings of trust and love. In East Asia, showing such feelings of affection and gentleness toward others is spoken of as "benevolence." And since olden times in Japan, the phrase "medicine is a benevolent art" has been used to express the essential nature of what it means to be a physician. It seemed to me that Dr. Nakamura, with his inborn temperament, was someone who knew the art of demonstrating human love in its most universal and fundamental form. In one of our interviews, he spoke some words that clearly illustrated how he viewed humans. This quote is a little lengthy, but I would like to reproduce it in full here:

Afghanistan is a country with extremely diverse people, diverse clans, diverse ethnic groups, and diverse classes, and they all skillfully manage to live together. One of their traditions is to somehow reach compromises that allow them to live together without friction. That's a hallmark of this country. At first, as a bystander you may think, "They're quite incompatible with us," or "These people are quite different from us." But once you get closer to them, you come to realize, "Oh, these people are not so different after all." Take thievery, for example. When people in Japan steal, it's often because they've lost all their money gambling on horse races or something, or because they want cash to pay for having some fun. But in Afghanistan, such cases are pretty rare. In this society, those who steal often do so because they don't want their children to go hungry the next day. Petty thievery of this sort is quite common, and it's a society where people turn a blind eye to it. When I think about that, it somehow gives me a warm feeling. True, while living here I've been betrayed by people, I've been robbed, and various other things have happened to me. But I strongly believe that good intentions are something that we all share, and that one can trust them. They exist in everyone. I have a feeling that they can even be found in a person who commits murder. Conversely, I also think that no matter how good someone may be, there are shadows within them, too. Putting it all together, I think that humans are worthy of our love and that their well-intentioned hearts are worthy of our trust.

Reconciliation of Humans and Nature

It is April 2019. Bathed by the strong rays of the Afghan sun, I am standing atop a hill next to the Marwarid Canal that Dr. Nakamura built. A vivid green stretch of land spreads before my eyes, and my soul is gladdened. It has been three and a half years since my last reporting trip to Afghanistan. On that last visit, I stood on the same hill and saw that this land was already covered in green. However, now I sense that something is a little different from that previous trip. It does not take long for me to realize that the difference is sound. I can now hear a variety of sounds carried by the winds blowing across the verdant landscape. I hear the spirited voices of the men at work, the happy cries of children playing, the lowing of cattle and the clucking of chickens, the chirping of songbirds. These sounds and the beautiful verdure serve as signs of robust life, and I feel overwhelmed by them. My soul is stirred when I realize that a genuine farm village has been brought back to life. It hits home to me that the people there are living the serene lives that Dr. Nakamura had envisioned and wanted to create.

At the same time, I also recall other things that I have seen. I began making a record of Dr. Nakamura's work in 1998, and over the course of my repeated visits to Afghanistan during the intervening twenty-one years, I have seen the changes to this land. Previously, it was an area assailed by drought and war, left totally bereft of any signs of life. I filmed scenes of people at their wits' end amid the cracked earth in a waterless hell; I recorded US Army helicopters flying overhead and armored vehicles speeding across the wasteland. In those years, who could have imagined that this barren stretch would be reborn as a lush and fertile land?

Today, the PMS irrigation channels have blended in with their natural surroundings, and they peacefully carry water along, almost as if they have been delivering water without interruption for centuries. Meanwhile, I keep thinking of one thing that Dr. Nakamura had quietly been talking about for ten years already, and which I had repeatedly taken note of: the "reconciliation of humans and nature." I heard him say that phrase over and over in both Afghanistan and Japan. However, the real meaning of his words was hard to grasp. What does it mean for humans and nature to reconcile? Not "humans protect nature," or "humans and nature coexist," but "humans and nature reconcile."

I decided to ask him about it. "When you speak of humans and nature 'reconciling,' what sort of thing do you mean?" He responded, "I think Nature should be seen as having personhood. That's why I use the word 'reconcile.'" What I think he was saying is this: If you see nature as an unresponsive mass, then humans can steal its bounty just as they please. However, if you see it as having personhood, then you engage in dialogue with it and encourage it to allow you to share a portion of its bounty. Furthermore, if you keep communicating with Nature when it is wounded, when it recovers humans will once again be able to share in its bounty. Simplistic though this may be, this is how I understood "reconciliation of humans and Nature." I also got the sense that the reconciliation of humans with Nature gives rise to hopes for the future. Right now, we are facing disheartening social conditions and anxieties about the future. In times like these, I think I am not the only one who sees strong hope for the future in the work that Dr. Nakamura continued to do and in the things he said.

As I again stood on that hill near the Marwarid Canal and looked once more at the verdant plain during my 2019 reporting trip, I realized that this is precisely what the reconciliation of humans and Nature means.

After Dr. Nakamura died, I reread the things that he had written, along with the newsletters of the Peshawar-kai, over and over again. I was reminded again that they are a treasure trove of his deep thoughts and his predictions for the future. Among them, I came across a passage that I particularly like. I have ruminated over it for a long time, and I am impressed with its depth of meaning:

> What will we leave behind for the next generation? When I consider the actions of those who were lost in the endless scorching winds, I think of the destination to which we are heading as being like a mirage. The rifles and the tanks, the indiscriminate slaughter, the bloody revels of foolish humans, the dreams of riches and honors regardless of due, people's flowery words—these, too, are all illusions. Now, as we try to turn this desert into grasslands, the fact that trees grow profusely here, that sheep rest near water, that fruit ripens in abundance, and that we have enabled all manner of living things to live here harmoniously is definite proof of grace.

In this world dominated by politicians unworthy of trust and humans who are wide awake only to their own interests, I can feel in my bones how much courage and hope Dr. Nakamura gave us with his actions and thoughts—and above all with the way he lived. Even if the names "PMS" and "Nakamura Tetsu" are someday forgotten, the green ground that Dr. Nakamura and his Afghan colleagues restored and the canal they built will still protect people for centuries to come and continue to help them live.

Chronologies: Afghanistan and Nakamura Tetsu

Year		Afghanistan		Nakamura Tetsu and Peshawar-kai
1838	Oct.	First Anglo-Afghan War begins.		
1878	Nov.	Second Anglo-Afghan War begins.		
1893	Nov.	Durand Line demarcates border with British India.		
1907			Jan.	Uncle Hino Ashihei (given name: Tamai Katsunori) born (d. 1960).
1919	May	Third Anglo-Afghan War begins.		
	Aug.	Treaty of Rawalpindi concluded, liberated from being British protectorate.		
1946			Sept.	Born in Fukuoka Prefecture.
1947	Aug.	India and Pakistan win independence from the United Kingdom.		
1963	Mar.	Prime Minister Daoud resigns.		
1964	Oct.	New constitution promulgated.		
1973	Jul.	Former Prime Minister Daoud seizes power in bloodless coup d'état and founds Republic of Afghanistan. Becomes president and abolishes the 1964 constitution.	Mar.	Graduates from Kyushu University School of Medicine and joins staff of the National Hizen Psychiatric Center.
1975				Joins staff of Ōmuta Rōsai Hospital (serves through 1978).
1978	Apr.	Saur Revolution occurs; President Daoud and his family executed. Democratic Republic of Afghanistan established.	Jun.	Goes to Pakistan as the group physician for the Fukuoka Mountaineering Club's Tirich Mir expedition. Also accepts a position at a neurosurgical hospital in the town of Hirokawa in the Yame district (holds post through 1982).
1979	Sept.	Amin Cabinet formed.		
	Dec.	Soviet Union begins invasion, outbreak of Soviet-Afghan War (lasts until 1989). President Amin assassinated. Karmal administration formed with Soviet backing.		
1983			Apr.	Japan Overseas Christian Medical Service (JOCS) decides to dispatch Nakamura to Peshawar.
			Sept.	Peshawar-kai founded.
			Dec.	First issue of the Peshawar-kai's newsletter published.

Year		Afghanistan		Nakamura Tetsu and Peshawar-kai
1984			May	Joins the Mission Hospital Peshawar in order to treat patients with Hansen's disease.
1985	Jan.	US government announces it will provide approximately US$280 million in aid to the mujahideen.		
	Mar.	Mikhail Gorbachev becomes general secretary of the Communist Party of the Soviet Union.		
1986			Apr.	Opens a sandal workshop at the hospital.
			Oct.	Establishes Afghan Leprosy Services (ALS) (formally founded the following April with help from Peshawar-kai).
1987			Jan.	Leading ALS, begins mobile care services for Afghan refugee camps around Pakistan's North-West Frontier Province.
1988	Apr.	Pakistan, Afghanistan, the United States, and the Soviet Union sign the Geneva Accords, agreeing on the withdrawal of Soviet troops.		
1989	Feb.	Soviet army completes its withdrawal. Civil war erupts between government forces and anti-Soviet guerrillas.	Jan.	ALS changes name to Japan-Afghan Medical Services (JAMS) and begins offering medical care in regions of Afghanistan that lack physicians.
1990			Jun.	Finishes his two-term stint with JOCS, around seven years total.
1991	Jan.	Gulf War begins.		
	Dec.	Soviet Union collapses.	Dec.	Opens first clinic in Afghanistan in Dara-e-Noor.
1992	Apr.	Anti-government forces capture Kabul, found Islamic State of Afghanistan.		
	May	Afghan refugees spontaneously begin to return home.	Dec.	Opens Dara-e-Pech Clinic.
1994	Jan.	Civil war intensifies, fighting in all parts of Afghanistan.	Apr.	Opens Wama Clinic.
	Nov.	Taliban bring Kandahar under their control.	Nov.	Establishes Peshawar Leprosy Services (PLS) Hospital as the base for medical activities.

Year		Afghanistan		Nakamura Tetsu and Peshawar-kai
1996	Sept.	Taliban seize Kabul, execute President Najibullah.		
	Oct.	Anti-Taliban factions create Northern Alliance.		
1997	Oct.	Taliban announce change of country's name to Islamic Emirate of Afghanistan.		
1998	Aug.	US carries out cruise missile strikes on suspected terrorist training camps.	Apr.	Founds PMS hospital by integrating PLS and JAMS; becomes executive director.
	Sept.	Taliban bring almost all of Afghanistan under their control.		
1999	Jul.	US presidential directive imposes economic sanctions on the Taliban regime.		
	Nov.	UN imposes first round of economic sanctions on the Taliban.		
2000	Jun.	Suffering from great drought grows. Taliban ban poppy cultivation.	Jul.	Projects to secure water supplies begin, including excavation and restoration of wells.
2001	Jan.	UN imposes second round of economic sanctions.		
	Mar.	Taliban destroy the Buddhas of Bamyan.	Mar.	Opens temporary clinics in five locations around Kabul.
	Sept.	September 11 terrorist attacks on New York and Washington, DC.	Jun.	Work begins on large wells for irrigation purposes in Dara-e-Noor.
	Oct.	US and UK begin massive air strikes. Japan passes Anti-Terrorism Special Measures Law.	Oct.	Planning of food supply program begins. Peshawar-kai announces establishment of "Afghan Fund for Life," which provides food for 270,000 people in Kabul to survive for three months. Nakamura attends Anti-Terrorism Special Measures Committee session of Japan House of Representatives as unsworn witness.
	Nov.	Japan Maritime Self-Defense Force vessels dispatched to the Indian Ocean. Northern Alliance seizes Kabul; Taliban regime collapses.		
	Dec.	Afghan Interim Authority formed at Bonn Conference; Hamid Karzai becomes chairman.		

Year		Afghanistan		Nakamura Tetsu and Peshawar-kai
2002	Jan.	Tokyo Conference on Afghanistan held.	Feb.	PMS announces its Green Ground Project.
	Mar.	UNHCR begins program to send Afghan refugees and internationally displaced persons home.	Jun.	PMS establishes office in Jalalabad to coordinate all projects related to medical services, water resource management, and farming.
			Aug.	Peshawar-kai receives 1st Okinawa Peace Prize.
2003	Jun.	*Loya jirga* (national assembly) convened in Kabul; Hamid Karzai elected president. Rents in Kabul rise steeply.	Feb.	Plan formulated to dig 13-kilometer-long irrigation canal in Kuz Kunar.
	Mar.	Iraq War begins.	Mar.	Groundbreaking ceremony for Marwarid Canal held.
			Aug.	PMS Dara-e-Pech Clinic is rebuilt with money from the Okinawan Peace Price; name is changed to Okinawa Peace Dara-e-Pech Clinic. Nakamura receives a Peace and International Understanding Citation from the Philippines' Ramon Magsaysay Award Foundation.
2004	Oct.	Presidential election held.	May	Number of wells dug exceeds 1,000.
	Dec.	Karzai regime formally launched.		
2005			Jan.	PMS temporarily closes clinics in Dara-e-Pech and Wama.
2006			Mar.	Irrigation canal goes beyond 10 kilometers in length.
			Apr.	Number of wells dug reaches 1,600; *karez* (lateral wells) completed in 38 places. All projects to develop sources of drinking water halted. Decision made to concentrate on irrigation projects (building canals and intake weirs).
2007	Nov.	Japan's Anti-Terrorism Special Measures Law expires.	Apr.	Phase one of Marwarid Canal construction completed (13 kilometers). Phase two of construction begins.
	Dec.	Pakistan's former prime minister Benazir Bhutto assassinated.	Oct.	Work begins to construct Sheiwa weir and restore river channel.
2008	Jan.	Japan enacts Replenishment Support Special Measures Law (revision of Anti-Terrorism Special Measures Law).	Feb.	Mosque and madrassa construction begins. Work on Sheiwa weir and water intake facilities completed.

Year		Afghanistan		Nakamura Tetsu and Peshawar-kai
	Mar.	Moves to dispatch Japan Ground Self-Defense Force put PMS on guard.	Mar.	Repatriation of Japanese workers begins.
			Aug.	Japanese worker Itō Kazuya abducted and killed.
			Oct.	Base of activities moved to Afghanistan.
			Nov.	Testifies before Committee on Foreign Affairs and Defense in Japan's Upper House. Repatriation of all Japanese workers is complete. Tree planting ceremony held at Gamberi Desert and erosion-control forest.
	Dec.	Replenishment Support Special Measures Law revised.	Dec.	Work begins on Kama I intake weir. Preparatory work begins for Behsud II intake weir.
2009	Mar.	US increases troop presence; number of troops involved with NATO's ISAF reaches 120,000.	Mar.	Dispute with US army's Provincial Reconstruction Team (PRT) over fish farm. Work on Behsud II intake weir halted due to PRT intervention.
			Apr.	Work begins on wetland treatment, drainage channel construction.
			Jul.	PMS Hospital (Peshawar) handed over to local NGO.
			Aug.	Marwarid Canal reaches its terminus.
2010	Feb.	Security conditions worsen dramatically.	Feb.	Completion ceremony held for Marwarid Canal (total length 25 kilometers), mosque, and madrassa.
	Aug.	Suicide bombings and other bombings increase sharply.	Aug.	Major flooding throughout Indus River region, 1,800 dead or missing. Irrigation canals burst in many locations, requiring improvements and repairs.
			Oct.	Work begins on Kama II intake weir and Behsud embankments (3.5 kilometers long) in collaboration with JICA. River channel at Sheiwa weir restored (1.8 kilometers long).

Year		Afghanistan		Nakamura Tetsu and Peshawar-kai
2011	Apr.	US increases air strikes by drones.	Apr.	Completion ceremony held for Kama I and Kama II intake weirs plus main canal (1 kilometer).
	May	US forces kill Osama bin Laden in Pakistan.		
	Jul.	ISAF begins transfer of responsibility for security to Afghan forces. Withdrawal of US forces begins.		
	Sept.	Former President Burhanuddin Rabbani assassinated, setback for government-led High Peace Council.	Aug.	Heavy localized downpours take place along Keshmand range. Major flash floods from Jaribaba Valley damage Marwarid and Kashkot canals. Repair work begins.
2012			Mar.	Work begins on bypass siphons for Shigi aqueduct and canal.
			Apr.	Completion ceremony for Behsud I weir and Behsud embankment.
	Sept.	US military announces completion of withdrawal of its expanded 33,000-troop dispatch.	Oct.	Work begins on Marwarid-Kashkot continuous weir and main canal (1.8 kilometers) in a collaboration with JICA to connect to Marwarid weir on opposite bank, creating continuous weir 505 meters wide.
2013	Jun.	ISAF completes transfer of security authority to Afghan forces. All of Afghanistan in state of anarchy. Opposition of Afghan government postpones peace talks between Taliban and US to be held in Qatar.	Jun.	Kashkot embankment (4 kilometers) completed. Number of trees planted reaches 750,000.
			Aug.	Major flood in eastern Afghanistan. Shigi aqueduct completed.
2014	Apr.	3rd Afghanistan presidential election and state assembly day.	Apr.	Livestock raising begins at the Gamberi pilot farm.
	May	Presidential election results announced: Abdullah Abdullah comes in first, Ashraf Ghani is runner-up.		
	Jun.	Presidential election runoff election held, with decisive vote between front-runners Abdullah and Ghani.		
	Aug.	US Secretary of State John Kerry makes surprise visit to Kabul to discuss next administration with Abdullah and Ghani.		

Year		Afghanistan		Nakamura Tetsu and Peshawar-kai
	Sept.	Abdullah and Ghani sign agreement to establish national unity government. Independent Election Commission announces that Ashraf Ghani is president-elect. Ghani takes office as president; Abdullah becomes chief executive. National unity government signs security agreement with US government. 12,000 people will continue to be stationed in Afghanistan after year-end, when International Security Assistance Force (ISAF) withdraws.	Sept.	Construction begins on Marwarid continuous weir (second JICA-PMS collaboration).
	Oct.	President Ghani visits Saudi Arabia on his first outing. President Ghani visits Beijing, China, for his second foreign trip. President Ghani participates in 4th Foreign Ministerial Conference of the Asian Core Countries (Istanbul Process) held in Beijing.	Oct.	Construction begins on Miran weir (third JICA-PMS collaboration).
	Dec.	Chief Executive Abdullah participates in Shanghai Cooperation Organization (SCO) meeting in Astana, Kazakhstan. Pakistan Taliban movement attacks military school in Peshawar, northwestern Pakistan, killing more than 130 children. ISAF completes its mission and withdrawal.	Dec.	Success in producing unrefined sugar from sugarcane grown on reclaimed land in the Gamberi Desert (revival of unrefined sugar production).
2015	Jan.	National unity government publishes list of all ministerial candidates. President Ghani and Chief Executive Abdullah nominate 13 and 12, respectively.		
	Feb.	Major out-of-season flood occurs in eastern Afghanistan. Water levels in the Kabul River exceed height of Behsud I inlet gate by 30 cm. Areas of Jalalabad inundated, snowfall and frequent avalanches in highlands, numbers of dead and missing rise.		

Year		Afghanistan		Nakamura Tetsu and Peshawar-kai
2015	Mar.	US President Barack Obama announces that he will maintain 9,800 US troops in the country at the end of 2015.		
	May	Informal talks between Afghan government and Taliban held in Doha, Qatar. Agreement is reached to establish a Taliban political office in Doha, Qatar.		
	Jun.	Informal talks between Afghan government and Taliban held in Oslo, Norway.		
	Jul.	Official peace talks between Afghan government and Taliban held in Murree, northern Pakistan. Taliban acknowledges that their leader Mullah Omar had actually died in 2013, and announces that Mullah Akhtar Mansour is to be his successor.		
	Sept.	Taliban occupies northern Kunduz city for three days.		
	Oct.	US military airstrikes on Doctors Without Borders hospital in Kunduz city kills forty-two people, including staff and patients.		
	Dec.	Fifth Ministerial Meeting of the Asian Core Countries, Istanbul Process and Ministerial Level Meeting held in Pakistan's capital, Islamabad. President Ghani attends. Chief Executive Abdullah attends SCO Summit held in China. Afghanistan approved for membership in the World Trade Organization (WTO). Indian Prime Minister Modi attends inauguration of Afghanistan's new parliament building.		

Year		Afghanistan		Nakamura Tetsu and Peshawar-kai
2016	Jan.	First round of four-party coordinated talks held in Islamabad, Pakistan with representatives from Afghanistan, Pakistan, the United States, and China gathering to resume peace talks with Taliban. Second four-party coordination talks held in Kabul. Taliban contacts Afghan government in Doha, Qatar.		
	Feb.	Third four-party coordination talks held in Islamabad. Fourth four-party coordination talks held in Kabul.	Feb.	Twenty-year lease signed for approximately 230 hectares of reclaimed land in the Gamberi Desert (Gamberi pilot farm).
	Mar.	UN Security Council unanimously votes to extend duration of UN Assistance Mission in Afghanistan. Yamamoto Tadamichi appointed as Special Representative of the UN Secretary-General for UN Assistance Mission in Afghanistan.	Mar.	Construction begins on main Gamberi drainage canal.
	May	Fifth four-party coordination talks held in Islamabad. Taliban leader Akhtar Mansour killed in Pakistani territory by US military drone strike. Hibatullah Akhundzada becomes Taliban leader.		
	Jul.	Pakistan government begins to forcibly repatriate Afghan refugees; 100,000 to 150,000 refugees go to Nangarhar Province.	Sept.	Construction completed on Miran weir (third JICA-PMS collaboration), guarantees stable irrigation for 1,700 hectares of land.
	Aug.	Militants take over American University in Kabul for over ten hours.	Oct.	To apply PMS water-intake system to a wider area, construction begins on Miran Training Center to cultivate human resources (PMS joint project with the Food and Agriculture Organization [FAO]). Construction begins on the Marwarid II weir (fourth JICA-PMS collaboration). First harvest of oranges at the Gamberi pilot farm.
	Dec.	Sixth Ministerial Meeting of the Istanbul Process Asian Core Country Conference held in Amritsar, India.		

Year		Afghanistan		Nakamura Tetsu and Peshawar-kai
2017	Jan.	UAE ambassador, senior government officials and others killed or injured in terrorist bomb attack on the official residence of the governor of Kandahar. Taliban calls on US President Trump to withdraw in a letter on the Internet.		
	Feb.	Second round of Afghanistan peace talks held in Moscow, Russia. Organization of Islamic Cooperation holds Afghanistan peace meeting in Jeddah, Saudi Arabia.		
	Mar.	Terrorists invade military hospital in Kabul and carry out terrorist attack, killing more than forty-nine people.	Mar.	464 date palms planted at the Gamberi pilot farm (joint project with the Embassy of Japan).
	Apr.	US forces drop massive MOAB bomb on IS stronghold in eastern Nangarhar province, killing more than ninety-four people. Third round of Russian-led peace talks in Afghanistan takes place in Moscow. US Defense Secretary Mattis becomes first Trump administration cabinet member to visit Afghanistan.	Apr.	PMS Afghan staff come to Japan for training from JICA. Nakamura begins to make it a policy to extend regular invitations for staff to go to Japan.
	May	Large-scale terrorist attack occurs in the embassy-heavy district of Kabul. More than 150 people are killed and more than 430 are injured.	May	PMS/Peshawar-kai lay out preparations to continue work for twenty more years.
	Aug.	President Trump announces new US strategy for South Asia.		
	Dec.	Seventh Istanbul Process Asian Core Countries Meeting held in Baku, Azerbaijan.	Nov.	Construction on Miran Training Center completed (joint FAO-PMS project).

Year		Afghanistan		Nakamura Tetsu and Peshawar-kai
2018	Jan.	Taliban attack and occupy the Intercontinental Hotel in Kabul. More than eighteen people, including fourteen foreigners, killed. More than 100 people killed in a terrorist attack in central Kabul.	Jan.	Classes begin at Miran Training Center (joint FAO-PMS project) as first step of a plan to spread the PMS water intake method.
	Feb.	Second meeting of the Kabul Process held.	Feb.	PMS and Nakamura awarded Afghanistan state medal of Ghazi Mir Masjidi Khan by President Ashraf Ghani.
	Mar.	First meeting on peace in Afghanistan held in Tashkent, Uzbekistan.		
	Jun.	Taliban agree to three-day cease-fire in conjunction with Muslim festival of Eid al-Fitr.	Jun.	Nakamura receives Japan Society of Civil Engineers' Outstanding Civil Engineering Achievement Award.
	Jul.	US Assistant Secretary of State Alice Wells meets directly with senior Taliban officials in Doha.		
	Sept.	US Army Commander John Nicholson retires; replaced by Commander Austin Miller. Former Ambassador Khalilzad appointed as US Special Envoy for Peace in Afghanistan.		
	Oct.	First direct negotiations between US and Taliban held in Doha. House of Representatives Election Day. Taliban founding member Mullah Baradar released from prison in Pakistan.	Oct.	Marwarid II weir project (fourth JICA-PMS collaboration) shifts to being under sole operation by PMS.
	Nov.	First peace talks with Taliban participation held in Moscow. Direct talks between US and Taliban in Doha.		
	Dec.	Pakistan-brokered Taliban-US peace talks held in Abu Dhabi, UAE. Taliban delegation meets with Iranian deputy foreign minister and others in Tehran, Iran.		

Year		Afghanistan		Nakamura Tetsu and Peshawar-kai
2019	Jan.	US-Taliban peace talks held in Doha. Mullah Baradar takes over as Taliban representative in peace talks. US Special Envoy for Peace Khalilzad announces agreement on the basic framework for peace talks with Taliban.		
	Feb.	US-Taliban peace talks held in Doha.	Mar.	Total number of trees planted reaches one million.
	Apr.	Supreme Court decides to grant President Ghani's term of office, which runs until 28th September. Grand assembly held to discuss peace negotiations with Taliban in Kabul.	Apr.	Beekeeping project begins at the Gamberi farm.
	May	US-Taliban peace talks held in Doha.	May	PMS and Nakamura publicly honored by Jalalabad Ulama (traditional religious council).
	Jun.	US-Taliban peace talks held in Doha.		
	Jul.	IS terrorist attack in Kabul, killing over fifty people.		
	Aug.	US-Taliban peace talks held in Doha. IS terrorist attack on wedding venue in Kabul kills more than eighty people.		
	Sept.	More than fifty civilians killed in airstrike by government and US forces in eastern Nangarhar Province. Presidential election day.		
	Oct.	Bombing at mosque in Nangarhar Province kills more than sixty-nine people.	Oct.	Nakamura granted honorary Afghan citizenship by President Ghani.
	Nov.	President Trump's first visit to Afghanistan since taking office.		
	Dec.	US-Taliban peace talks held in Doha.	Dec.	Nakamura killed by unknown assailants in Jalalabad as he heads to work. Peshawar-kai Chairman Murakami Masaru appointed general director of PMS.
2020			Feb.	First joint PMS–Peshawar-kai conference held in India.

INDEX

Note: Page numbers (excluding Roman numerals) in *italic* refer to photographs or illustrations. The abbreviation '*t*' refers to a table. *Frontispiece* refers to photographs near the title page at the front of the book.

hospital *see* Peace Japan Medical Services
Hospital

I

Industrial Patriotic Society 15
intake gates/weirs
  initial stages 85, 92, 94, *96*, 116, 134
  lessons from Great Flood 171–2, *173*,
    174–7, *178–9*
  withstanding floods/drought 161, *162*,
    163, *164*, 165, *166*, 167
international medical assistance 3, 31, 43,
  49, 51–2, 70, 182
International Medical Assistance Foundation *see* Fundação Assistência Médica
  Internacional (International Medical
  Assistance Foundation) (AMI)
International Red Cross 70, 182
International Security Assistance Force
  (ISAF) 77, 119, 140, 183
irrigation canal construction *see* Gamberi
  Desert (Phase Two); Marwarid irrigation
  canal (Phase One)
Irrigation Department (Nangarhar Province) 136, 137, *139*
ISAF *see* International Security Assistance
  Force
Islam and Islamist groups 8, 29, 31, 46, 59,
  104, *105*, *106*, 107
Itō Kazuya 115–16, *117*, 120, 132, 181

J

Jalalabad (Afghanistan) 7, 33, 60, 66, 70, 72,
  78, 79, 120, 194–5
JAMS *see* Japan-Afghanistan Medical
  Service
Japan 12, 33, 107, 116, 140, 142, 182, 186,
  200
  civil engineering techniques 87, 90–2, 94,
    96, 97, 145, 148
  connection to nature 183–5, 187–8
  military intervention 67, 68, 115

oblique weirs 95, *96*, 97, 161, 163, *164*,
  165
overseas development assistance (ODA)
  70, 73–4, 102, 176, 177
Japan International Cooperation Agency
  (JICA) 137, 156, 176–7
Japan Overseas Christian Medical Cooperative Service (JOCS) 31
Japan-Afghanistan Medical Service (JAMS)
  49, 51–52
Jaribaba 7, 85, 95
Jaspers, Karl 28
JICA *see* Japan International Cooperation
  Agency
"jihad" 48
jirga (autonomous assembly of community
  elders) 8, 11
JOCS *see* Japan Overseas Christian Medical
  Cooperative Service
jui (artifical water channels) *80*, 92

K

Kabul 59, 77, 82, 119
  opening of clinics 65, 66, 70, *71*, 72–3,
    74, 76
Kabul River 79, 177
Kakumei zengo (Before and after the revolution) (Hino) 15
Kama Canal 171–2, *173*, 174, 198
karez (horizontal well) 63, *64*, 79, *80*, 90
Karzai, Hamid 72, 73
Kashkot-Marwarid continuous weir 177,
  179
Khalid (engineer) 137
Khan, Delawal 137, *139*
Khan, Ikramullah 120, *139*, 140
Khan, Mohammed Daoud 46
Khyber Pakhtunkhwa *see* North-West
  Frontier Province
Khyber Pass 42–3, 51, 111
Kikkawa-san (local postmaster) 5, 20–1

World Health Organization (WHO) 59

Y

Yamada Oblique Weir (Chikugo River, Japan) 95, *96*, 97, 161, 163, *164*, 165

Yamada-zeki/Horikawa sanbyaku-gojū-nen shi (350 years of the Yamada Weir and the Horikawa Canal) 163

Yatsu Kenji 191–202

Z

Zaman, Noor *133*

Ziaur-Rahman, Dr. 70, *117*, 119, *121*, 122, 132, 137–8, *139*

About the Author

Nakamura Tetsu was born in 1946 in Fukuoka Prefecture and served as the physician and general director of Peace Japan Medical Services (PMS). He was a graduate of Kyushu University School of Medicine. Following work at medical facilities in Japan, he took a position in Peshawar, Pakistan, in 1984, and was involved thereafter in providing medical care to the impoverished, focusing on treating Hansen's disease. In 1986, he formed a team to provide medical care to Afghan refugees and also began providing care to mountain communities that lacked physicians. He opened three clinics in Afghanistan's mountainous eastern regions from 1991 onward, and opened PMS's base hospital in 1998. In 2000, in parallel with his medical services, he began digging and repairing wells to secure sources of water around Afghanistan, which was suffering from a massive drought. Between 2003 and 2009 he led the construction of a 25-kilometer-long irrigation canal. Dr. Nakamura continued to work at opening desert lands to farming in spite of having to contend with sandstorms and floods. He won numerous awards, including the Peace and International Understanding Citation from the Philippines' Ramon Magsaysay Award Foundation and the Fukuoka Prize. His written works include *Peshawāru nite* (At Peshawar), *I wa kokkyō o koete* (Medicine knows no borders), *Isha ido o horu* (A doctor digs wells), and *Isha, yōsuiro o hiraku* (A doctor builds a canal), all published by Sekifūsha.

Dr. Nakamura was killed by unknown assailants in Jalalabad, Afghanistan, in December 2019.

About the Translator

Carl Freire is a translator based in Tokyo. He is a graduate of Oberlin College and the University of Michigan, and also pursued doctoral studies in Japanese history at the University of California, Berkeley. In addition, he has worked as a journalist in Osaka and Tokyo.

（英文版）天、共に在り　　アフガニスタン三十年の闘い

Providence Was with Us: How a Japanese Doctor Turned the Afghan Desert Green

2020年12月4日　第1刷発行

著　者　　中村 哲
訳　者　　カール・フレーレ
発行所　　一般財団法人出版文化産業振興財団
　　　　　〒101-0051 東京都千代田区神田神保町2-2-30
　　　　　電話　03-5211-7283
　　　　　ホームページ　https://www.jpic.or.jp/

印刷・製本所　　大日本印刷株式会社